"Mark Traylor envisi— — — — — — —
in which we curren— — — — — — —
to live into. In Radicalizing — — —, — — —
theoretical framework for what such peace looks like and the practical steps to make peace a reality. I recommend it for everyone who wants to join God in bringing peace on Earth as it is in heaven!"

—Thomas Jay Oord

Author, *The Uncontrolling Love of God*

"Mark Traylor's words are full of light fun and joy, while still being encouraging and supportive at the deepest level. Throughout his *Radicalizing Peace*, he offers good, small, faithful steps that we can take to encourage peace. Not only are they smart, but they are actually attainable. I recommend taking a few minutes a day to read a section before heading out into the world. It will make it a better place for those you run into."

—Mike Malterre

Founder and Director, Parentteachercoach.com

"*Radicalizing Peace* is a short introduction to peace, but a great place for Christians to begin to rethink how we are called to be "peacemakers" in our troubled world today. As I look at the world, *Radicalizing Peace* is coming out at the right time, in the right way, for Christians to make a significant difference for peace in the name of Jesus Christ."

—Rev. Dr. Steven A. Tollefson

Pastor Emeritus, Cathedral of the Rockies

"*Radicalizing Peace* provides a thought-provoking discussion about what it means to be a peacemaker. As followers of the Prince of Peace, Christians have a mandate to work toward establishing peace. Yet far too often, well-intentioned individuals think and behave in ways that undermine the very peace we seek to promote. Traylor's insights provide an opportunity for us to examine how we may be contributing to the problem and, more importantly, specific actions we can take to more effectively contribute to the cure. The lessons drawn from *Radicalizing Peace* have the potential to better equip us to become the peacemakers we are called to be—and thereby change the world."

—Mary Olson

Ph.D. Lecturer, Boise State University,
College of Business and Economics

"Mark Traylor has done us all a great service. A student and a practitioner of peace, he wisely reminds us that peace is so much more than the absence of conflict. He also cautions that peace is not just an affair of the heart—peacemaking is hard work. It takes discipline, discernment, and dedication. The good news? We all can and should become peacemakers, and Traylor shows us how, theoretically and practically. Read this book and put your peacemaking skills to work!"

—Steve Shaw

Ph.D. Professor, Political Science, and Director,
Honors College at Northwest Nazarene University

RADICALIZING PEACE

Jeanne & Wayne
   I love + appreciate you guys so much! Thanks for teaching me about the peaceful example of Jesus

Mel Taylor

RADICALIZING PEACE

How Your **Good, Small, Faithful Steps** Can Change the World

MARK TRAYLOR

elevate faith

Copyright © 2016 by Mark Traylor

All rights reserved. No portion of this book may be reproduced, stored in a retrieval system, or transmitted in any form or by any means © electronic, mechanical, photocopy, recording, scanning, or other © except for brief quotations in critical reviews or articles, without the prior written permission of the publisher.

Scripture quotations are taken from various versions of the Bible, noted after each use. Used by permission.

Published in Boise, Idaho by Elevate Faith,
a division of Elevate Publishing.

Web: www.elevatepub.com

Editorial work: AnnaMarie McHargue

Cover design: Aaron Snethen

This book may be purchased in bulk for educational, business, ministry, or promotional use.

Library of Congress Control Number: 2016942323

ISBN (print): 9781943425976
ISBN (e-book): 9781943425983

This book is dedicated to my children, Carlie, Hailie, and Zac, with a passionate desire that they might live in a more peaceful, harmonious, and joyous world.

Acknowledgments

I would like to express my deepest gratitude for my good friend and editor, Anna McHargue, for encouraging me to write this book and for keeping me inspired and motivated along the way. I would also like to thank Melodie Galyon for the solid research she provided and the wisdom she offered during my writing process.

Contents

One: How Your Good, Small, Faithful Steps Can Change the World 1

"Peace" Is a Major Bible Theme. 3
It's a Mandate 6
It All Starts at Home 9

Two: Humility—The Prerequisite for Peace 13

Incomplete Stories. 15
We Know Just Enough to Be Dangerous 17
Getting a Little Humility about the "Christian
    Worldview". 21
The Problem with Being Absolutely Sure. 23

Three: In Defense of Kindness 27

Gotta Be Right 30
Being Correct about Political Correctness. 32
Learning to Play Nice 34

Four: No Forgiveness, No Peace 37

Forgive Us Our Debts, Trespasses, Sins…Whatever. 38
Father, Forgive Us 40

Gather Your Courage and Ask for Forgiveness.......... 41
Do Yourself a Favor and Forgive Your Debtor 46
Forgiveness Is a Process 49
Amazing Grace 51

Five: Peacemaking Is Risky Business 55

Irrational Fears...................................... 57
An Opportunity to Take a Risk for Peace 60

Six: Why Being a Prophet for Peace Will Be Unpopular 67

The Prophets of the Old Testament 69
Peacemakers Will Love Their Enemies
  and Challenge Their Friends....................... 73
Speak Up for Your Enemies.......................... 77

Seven: The Other Side of the Road: Racial Attitudes and Peacemaking 81

What's Yours Is Mine—I'll Take It.................... 85
What's Mine Is Mine—I'll Keep It.................... 86
Cleaning Up the Mess............................... 89
What's Mine Is Yours—I'll Share It................... 89
Going Out of Our Way............................... 92

Eight: Making It Happen—Practical Steps Toward Radicalizing Peace 95

1. Start a Small Home Book or Study Group Focused on Peace 97
2. Donate to a Peacemaking Group That You Believe In and Trust 99
3. Lobby Your Legislators........................... 101
4. Participate in Peaceful Protests.................... 104
5. Go Overseas on a Short-Term Development Project.. 109

Encouraging Peace: An Overview....................117
About the Author 119

ONE

How Your Good, Small, Faithful Steps Can Change the World

Throughout Scripture, we find passages that raise our hopes and aspirations and cause us to believe that God desires the very best for His Creation. Certainly one of the most inspirational among these is the promise given by the angels on the occasion of Jesus' birth. After appearing to the shepherds, the angels proclaimed, "Glory to God in the highest, and on earth peace, good will toward men." *(Luke 2:14)*

So whatever happened with that whole "peace" deal? Where'd that go? Peace on earth, good will toward men? Well, thanks for sending us that message, Lord. It sure made the shepherds feel good at the time. We still like to sing about it at Christmas. But where is the follow-through?

Almost immediately after the angels made this announcement, peace was completely shattered for the people of the region. Herod got wind of a new "King of the Jews." He went on a violent rampage to eliminate the competition by brutally killing all of the male infants in his jurisdiction. Throughout the lifetime of the "Prince of Peace," Roman atrocities such as these continued unabated.

Since then, things have only gotten worse. Mankind continuously has had to endure civil wars, conquests, coups, border conflicts, world wars, race wars, and genocide. In recent times, we've suffered through the horrors of 9/11, the wars in Afghanistan and Iraq, the disintegration of nations like Syria, the rise of extremist groups like Al-Qaeda and ISIS, and the spread of terrorist attacks on civilian targets. Mass shootings have become routine, and we expect to hear about a new incident every week.

As a result of this, whenever religious people speak about peace, they play down the expectations with watered-down variations on the theme. They talk about inner peace, peace of mind, peace with God, marital peace, and peace with your in-laws (good luck with that!).

But what about peace on earth? Wasn't *that* the promise of the angels?

But how can we even engage in a conversation about peace when we ourselves—Christians—are routinely squabbling? We're in conflict with people who hold different opinions or practice a different religion. If that isn't enough, we even tangle with people who attend our own churches. In our relationships with family, co-workers, and neighbors, Christians don't seem to be better than anyone else at making peace. In fact, Christians often appear to be more cantankerous and combative than the population at large. How have we let this happen?

As people of faith, all of this should concern us greatly. Somehow, because we are the representatives of the Prince of Peace here on Earth, we need to figure out how we can start to make a difference—how our good, small, faithful steps can bring the world a tiny bit closer to the world of peace promised by the angels.

"PEACE" IS A MAJOR BIBLE THEME

Peace is a key theme of Biblical teaching and emphasis. The coming of the Messiah is the coming of peace. The prophet Isaiah proclaimed that the Messiah would be the Prince of Peace, and that swords would one day be beaten into plowshares and spears into pruning hooks. Jesus declared, "Blessed are the peacemakers" *(Matthew 5:9)* and also, "Peace, I leave you; my peace I give you." *(John 14:27)* The apostle Paul admonished us to "let the peace of Christ rule and reign in our hearts." *(Colossians 3:15)* Peter implored us to "seek peace and pursue it." *(1 Peter 3:11)*

Now, it's clear that as the Bible describes it, complete peace will not be fully realized until the end of history. The lion does not lie down with the lamb until the story ends.

But God's intention for the present is also clear. The Bible describes peace as a good thing: a condition to be desired and striven for. And there is no doubt that His people are supposed to be peacemakers. In the Bible, peace is a "thing," a big deal.

And yet there are some people—Christians and non-Christians alike—who think that all this "peace talk" is some kind of leftist conspiracy. They believe that "peace" is a code word for a liberal agenda. All that "peace talk" is just for hippies and vegans and Norwegians and people like that.

But peace is not a red state/blue state thing. Peace is a Bible word. It doesn't belong to one side or the other. The idea of peace represents a challenge, both to those who lean left and to those who lean right. We have a moral and a spiritual obligation to pursue it, no matter our political ideology.

So, if you lean a little to the right, don't abandon this central Biblical aspiration just because you think the whole "peace vibe" thing doesn't jive with your politics. If you label every effort at diplomacy as weakness, and decry every negotiation as appeasement, and want to charge into every conflict like Rambo with guns a-blazing, then you have to ask yourself if you are really representing the Prince of Peace.

In recent years, interestingly enough, Christians have been among those who have argued most consistently and vociferously for aggressive military action toward our enemies.

On the other hand, if you lean a little to the left, and think of yourself as a peacenik, there are still questions that you need to ask as well—because it's easy to oversimplify and idealize the road to peace. There is a dysfunctional kind of peacemaking that avoids conflict and sweeps big problems under the rug. It confuses the proper relationship between forgiveness and justice. It leaves the perpetrators of violence or corruption unpunished and leaves the injured vulnerable to future harm.

Dysfunctional peacemaking pretends everything is fine and advocates for oversimplified, superficial, "make nice" solutions. It leaves old resentments to fester and grow worse.

Maybe you have some of these dysfunctional peacemakers in your family. Maybe *you're* the dysfunctional peacemaker! You just want everybody to get along. Tension makes you cringe. You encourage your sister to avoid the topics of religion or politics. And you tell your kids, whatever they do, don't mention uncle Bob's comb-over!

But effective peacemaking is never about sweeping things under the rug, and it's never about avoidance. Real peacemaking is about a commitment to do the really hard work of understanding and helping others to understand one another. It means you're going to get your hands dirty. It means you're going to make some people uncomfortable, and it means that you, yourself, will be uncomfortable for long periods of time. It requires a firm dedication to digging deep and uncovering root problems, rather than settling for short-term, superficial, Band-Aid-type approaches. Real peacemaking comes with heavy emotional, spiritual, and financial costs. Sometimes it costs lives. It might even cost you yours. Always, it costs you your pride. Count on that.

IT'S A MANDATE

In December 2013 I heard a sermon delivered by the influential Pastor Bill Hybels. It was a stirring call for Christians to become peacemakers, not just in our homes and our neighborhoods and communities, but in the world. This message challenged me to get serious about peacemaking in a way that I had never been challenged before in 56 years of Christian experience. Bill made it clear that being a peacemaker is an obligation for all who call themselves followers of Christ. It was the call that stimulated my interest and passion around this issue.

Hybels pointed out that both peacemaking and warmaking are strategy-intensive endeavors. When top military leaders think about going to war, it necessitates a lot of planning and preparation. There are so many logistical challenges that must be addressed. Strategists have to weigh options and make plans. I always envision a group of generals standing around a big map table in a bunker, using sticks to move around little tanks and army men. Today, of course, it's a more computerized process, involving GPS mapping and sophisticated algorithms.

The same level of planning, preparing, and strategizing must also be applied in effective peacemaking operations. It requires hours and weeks and months, and sometimes years of careful and intensive work. It's intense and exhausting and often risky. But are you willing?

In his message, Hybels reminded us that:

When Jesus said, "Blessed are the peacemakers" (Matthew 5:9), he was formally commissioning each and every one of His followers to do absolutely everything in their power to contribute to His vision of peace on Earth.

Jesus was volunteering all of us for a really difficult task. Now when your spouse does this, you might have every right to protest. But when Jesus volunteers you for a tough task without asking your permission, well, what can you say? He's the Master; we are the servants. He assigns the jobs. So if you're His follower, you're supposed to be a peacemaker. There really isn't much you can say about it. It's a time for obedience.

And it's not just you. It's me, too. I have to honestly ask myself, how seriously have I taken my peacemaking mandate? Because if I'm going to be any good at it, I'm going to have to start taking it more seriously. Truthfully, it's hard to know where to start.

During the course of my lifetime, I have never been taught or trained about how to be an effective Christian peacemaker. The issue simply has not been on the Christian radar. American Christians, on the whole, have not talked about peace, have not taught about peace, have not sung about peace, and have not labored for peace.

But as Christ's followers, we ought to be the world leaders on the issue of peacemaking. Fortunately, some Christians are showing the way. They are not well known, and their organizations are small and poorly funded. But they are out there. And we need to start by asking questions like, "What are these individuals and organizations doing? How can we encourage their work, and join them in it? What role could I play within one of these organizations? How could my church get involved?" We'll examine some of these questions later in this book.

These kinds of questions demand our attention. Because Jesus wants us to be the peacemakers. We can't just leave the work to professional diplomats and the political classes. Of course, their work is extremely important, but it clearly has not been enough. So what is the plan for peace? *We* are the plan for peace. I like what pastor Efrem Smith has to say about this: "When Jesus returns He will bring ultimate justice, but until then, it's just us!"

IT ALL STARTS AT HOME

The truth is no one from the State Department has been calling me to ask for my opinions or policy advice. I'm guessing you have not received that call either. But clearly, one of the biggest things that limits our policy makers, and ties their hands, is the heated and divided politics of our time. They can't do the things they know should be done because the political repercussions at home are just too severe.

Possibly, then, one of the biggest things we can do to encourage peace around the world is to be among those who create a more conciliatory and humble tone in our public discourse here at home.

Listen to how the apostle Paul described our role as facilitators of reconciliation: "God reconciled us to Himself through Christ and gave us the ministry of reconciliation. God was reconciling the world to Himself in Christ, not counting people's sins against them." *(2 Corinthians 5:19)*

You know what reconciliation is, right? Reconciliation occurs when two parties who have been in conflict are brought together and their relationship is restored. In other words, reconciliation is peacemaking.

And He has committed to us the message of reconciliation.

So we see it here again. Jesus has committed us to the job. You're in, whether you signed up for it or not. You've got a mandate.

We are therefore Christ's ambassadors as though God were making His appeal through us. *(2 Corinthians 5:20)*

And here is the key sentence. We are *ambassadors* for Christ. We are diplomats!

The Bible does not say that we are cowboys for Christ! Nowhere are we encouraged to be cowboys for Christ. Why do so many Christians want to act like cowboys? We are supposed to be Christ's ambassadors!

What do ambassadors do? They try to learn the language of the people across the table from them. They try to help people understand each other. They make an effort to tone things down, to keep things from escalating among parties with different opinions, interests, and agendas.

An ambassador uses diplomatic language when she or

he speaks with people on the other side of the table. An ambassador is not given to rants and tirades. That kind of behavior is unbecoming to a diplomat.

Some of us really need to learn how to play nice in our conversations with others, especially if we call ourselves Christ followers. Unfortunately, it has become all too common for Christians to use the most heated and hateful rhetoric against their opponents. We need to learn how to become peacemakers, how to become Christ's ministers of reconciliation. We need to keep in mind, in every conversation, that we represent the Prince of Peace.

We all need to play our little part in creating a more conciliatory tone in our little corner of the office, the neighborhood, and the nation. Christians simply cannot be the meanest, maddest, angriest ones out there. When we do that, we just become one more angry voice in a sea of angry voices. We do not honor the Prince of Peace when we speak in undiplomatic ways and forget our status as His ambassadors. When we are cowboys for Christ, we represent something else, something that has very little to do with Jesus Christ.

I like what the angels said: "Glory to God in the highest, and on Earth, peace, goodwill toward men." *(Luke 2:14)* That's good stuff! I like the poetry of it. But if that is ever going to be more than just poetry, and if any of it is really ever going to happen, I must recognize that it begins with me.

What Good, Small, Faithful Step Can I Take to Encourage Peace?

I can be a calm, quiet diplomat in
a crowd of angry cowboys.

TWO

Humility—The Prerequisite for Peace

In any and every situation where there is conflict, peace is not possible unless someone is willing to swallow his pride. The only way that two conflicting parties are ever going to come together is when people are willing to acknowledge that there are things they don't understand, things they don't know, and things they've gotten wrong.

Over the years, I have had a lot of opportunity to travel overseas. Most of this travel has been in the context of our church's mission work. Once a year for the past 30 years, I have traveled to places like Mexico, Guatemala, and Kenya where we have established long-term development projects in impoverished rural communities.

This type of travel is so different from what we normally think of as vacation travel. It puts you in touch with the real problems and challenges of people who live in a world that is very different than our own.

Mark Twain noted, "Travel is fatal to prejudice, bigotry, and narrow-mindedness, and many of our people need it sorely on these accounts. Broad, wholesome, charitable views of men and things cannot be acquired by vegetating in one little corner of the earth all of one's lifetime."

People will often ask me about our mission trips to these faraway places. They say things like, "Why not take all the money that you're spending to travel to Kenya or Guatemala or wherever, and just send that money to be spent directly on the projects? Travel costs are so high. Isn't that money better spent by staying at home and applying the funds directly to your development work?"

These are good questions, and there are a couple of ways that I would answer. First, you have to recognize that if people didn't travel to these locations, they would not give an amount equal to what they would have spent had they gone. They would not donate the $3,000 it would take to get to Kenya, for example. Instead, they would donate $200 to the project, which is great, but would not provide the kind of funding that the question assumes. In fact, if they *do* go, they are much more likely to become lifelong donors to projects in that region.

But more importantly, the question misses the main point for taking the trip. We go to get a bigger, more global perspective, and a more complete picture of the world. These trips are life-changing experiences for the people who go. It broadens us, changes us, deepens our insight, challenges our assumptions, and makes us smarter.

People will also ask, "So, what has all this travel taught you over the years? What is the biggest lesson you've learned?" Well I can answer that question in four words: *I don't know nuthin'!*

The more I travel, and the more I get to know people who are different from me, the more I realize how big this world is, and how limited my exposure has been. I begin to get a glimpse of the great big world beyond the small little bubble where I live, and I start to see how narrow and inaccurate my worldview is. The more I travel, the more I see how little I actually know or understand.

INCOMPLETE STORIES

When I was in elementary school, I was not a great student. So anytime I did something that I was proud of, I remember it because it happened so infrequently.

I particularly remember one assignment to write a report about Africa. As I studied the words and pictures in our ancient copy of the E*ncyclopedia Britannica*, I became fascinated. I copied down the most interesting facts for my paper, and even took the initiative to draw some pictures to go with my text. I recall one drawing of a leopard that I was particularly proud of.

I had such a sense of satisfaction when I turned that report in to my teacher. Like Ralphie from the movie *Christmas Story*, I, too, was confident that I finally was going to get an A+. But, like Ralphie, I ended up with a similar result.

You can only imagine my dismay when my report came back graded as "incomplete." Incomplete was the worst grade that a kid could get. It meant that you had to go back and do more work. At least with a bad grade, you could just put it all behind you and move on.

Apparently, I hadn't followed the instructions for the assignment, and I hadn't included information the teacher had requested. She wanted to know about the region's populations, history, and natural resources. But I considered that kind of information boring and irrelevant. Who cared about all that? I had a picture of a leopard, for crying out loud!

I remember feeling both offended and insulted by her "incomplete," marked in angry red pencil at the top corner of my paper. How *dare* she say it was incomplete!

Well, during the course of the last decade traveling to Africa, I realize that the story I had told myself about that place is, indeed, incomplete. In fact, it remains incomplete even after all the years and experiences I've had there.

We all like to think that we understand the world. But this is a myth. We lack the perspective that can only be gained when we see through the eyes of others. We all tell ourselves a story about how the world works, about how it operates, and about who's good and who's bad. In the process, we invent a fable. We write for ourselves a false narrative. It is an oversimplified story that reduces a deeply complex planet to simple formulaic stereotypes. We do this because it is a natural instinct. We all want to make sense of the world so that we can feel good about our place in it.

But we are only kidding ourselves. The stories we invent are only relevant and convenient to our personal situation. We create a narrative that matches up with our ideology, that justifies our lifestyle, which validates who *we* are and what *we* do. Isn't it convenient that our view of the world makes us feel good about ourselves? A happy coincidence, I guess.

And if someone dare tell us that our story is incomplete or inaccurate, we get really offended and insulted. How *dare* they challenge our view of the world?

We all have to realize that the stories we tell ourselves about other peoples and other places are incomplete at best, and purposely self-serving at worst.

WE KNOW JUST ENOUGH TO BE DANGEROUS

There's another trap we Christians fall into: we can't convince ourselves that travel and international experience will make our stories complete. If travel and experience are really doing their job, then they should serve to make us more aware of our ignorance. But sometimes, travel can have the opposite effect. It can turn people into "know-it-alls."

We've all heard from people who've taken a two-week vacation and come back as "experts" on the place they have just visited. They will say things like, "Yeah, I just spent two weeks in Israel, so I know all about the Israeli-Palestinian conflict and why they have fought for so long." Really?

I remember that after my freshman year in college, I knew everything. What a wonderful feeling that was! I came home from school telling my dad how the world worked, and how all the most complicated problems could be solved. I had read a few poets, studied a few philosophers, and digested a few books. Everything had become so clear and simple. Now I was able to come home and straighten out the old man.

My dad listened for a while and then said to me, "You know just enough to be dangerous." And it was true. I knew just enough to form opinions, but not enough to form good ones. I knew just enough to think that I could offer solutions that would do nothing but make things worse. I knew just enough to charge ahead in blind arrogance and do some real damage. I knew just enough to be a much bigger idiot than I would've been if I had realized that I knew nothing at all.

First Corinthians 13 is a well-known passage that is often called "The Love Chapter" because of its beautiful and poetic description of what it really means to love. But often overlooked is a brilliant insight it provides about human knowledge.

> Where there are prophecies, they will cease; where there are tongues, they will be stilled; where there is knowledge, it will pass away.

Well, thank goodness for that. It sounds like the end of cable news!

> For now we know in part and we prophesy in part, but when completeness comes, what is in part disappears. *(1 Corinthians 13:8-9)*

One day we'll get the story right, and we'll complete our reports...but that day is not today.

> For now we see only a reflection as in a mirror; [The King James version says, "Now we see in a glass darkly."] then we shall see face to face. Now I know in part; then I shall know fully, even as I am fully known. *(1 Corinthians 13:12)*

It's saying, "I don't even understand myself. I think I do, but I don't even have a clear picture of who I am, let alone the rest of the world."

We all have only a partial, limited view of the way things are. We all see only a dim reflection in a glass darkly.

Why do witnesses to the same accident report events so differently? Are they lying? No, it's just that they saw the accident from a different vantage point, a different angle, a different location. Why is the umpire accused of being blind? Because things look differently in the stands than they do on the field. Not to mention, by the way, that fans—people—only see what they want to see.

Why does management appear mean-spirited to workers, and workers appear whiney to management? Why do liberals seem so naïve to conservatives, and conservatives seem both narrow-minded and hardhearted to liberals? Why do blacks see police actions and criminal justice proceedings so differently than whites?

It's because they're looking at things from a different angle, a different viewpoint, a different place, a different location. In short, they have a different point of view.

And here is the key thing to understand if you would be a peacemaker and an ambassador of reconciliation for Christ:

If you were standing where they are standing, then you would see what they see.

So peacemakers know that they have to go and stand where the other is standing. This is why we travel, instead of just sending money. This is why we must travel within our own country. We need to travel down the street, across the tracks, to the other side of town. We have to go to our neighbor's house and see how different our backyard looks compared to his backyard. We need to go and talk to the people who work in other departments within our company, or maybe even talk to the guy in the next cubicle.

Because peacemakers understand that they don't know everything. They understand that, in fact, <u>they don't know anything, unless they make an effort to learn from someone else's point of view.</u>

GETTING A LITTLE HUMILITY ABOUT THE "CHRISTIAN WORLDVIEW"

Today, in evangelical circles, you hear a lot of talk about the "Christian Worldview." The idea is that because Christians view the world through the lens of Scripture, they can see the world more rightly and accurately than other people. They believe the Bible gives them a "God's-eye" view, which is a far more accurate view than others who do not adopt a Scriptural viewpoint.

In other words…they're right and everybody else is wrong. They believe that they see things clearly, that their version of the story is complete. They give themselves an A+.

But that worldview, as they express it, is not the same worldview that is held by all Christians. It is not a worldview that is held by others who study and honor the Bible. The fact is the worldview expressed by so many American evangelicals is actually a pretty American view, held by a pretty conservative group of Americans. It's not a worldview shared by other Christians in other parts of the world. Even Christians in this country do not have a monolithic worldview, despite the fact that they are all trying to see the world through the lens of Scripture.

Most importantly, it is essential to realize that the worldview held today by those who espouse the Christian worldview has not been the worldview of Christians at other times in history.

In earlier days, slavery was an important part of the Christian worldview. Christians saw it as Biblically ordained, and they felt that the Bible was clear on the matter.

Through most of Christian history, the Christian worldview was to view women as property. Their role was to bear children and stay in the kitchen. They quoted a number of Bible verses to make this clear. That was the Christian worldview!

It was the Christian worldview that you burn people at the stake if they dare to disagree. It was the Christian worldview that "savages" should be subjugated and forced to become Christians or die.

People who espouse the Christian worldview have said and will say,

"Oh, yes yes, but we have all that behind us now. We've realized those mistakes and moved beyond them. Now, at this particular point in history, we finally have arrived at a complete and accurate Biblical worldview. Now, we've got it right."

Hmmm, really?

As far as I can see, the people who like to talk about the Christian worldview all come from just one small corner of the world. They tell one, narrow, convenient, overly simplistic story. They ignore the ideas of other people who also take the Bible seriously. It is a worldview that ignores history and forgets the flaws and failures of our Christian past. It carries a distinct Anglo-American cultural bias. It discounts other points of view. It is profoundly incomplete.

Remember the words of the Apostle Paul: "Now we see as in a glass darkly…now we know *in part*, and prophesy *in part*." *(1 Corinthians 13:12,* emphasis mine)

So maybe we need to get a little humility about our Christian worldview.

THE PROBLEM WITH BEING ABSOLUTELY SURE

We are living in a time, maybe more than any other time, when so many people are so *deeply* opinionated about so many things. We constantly encounter people who hold such strident, dogmatic views. It's become impossible to avoid them!

Maybe this is because we live in the Information Age. So many of us have become addicted to the 24-hour news cycle. We take in a lot of information. We are in front of the television, watching our preferred version of the news, for 10, 15, 20, maybe 30 hours a week. We've got a *lot* of information!

As a result, many of us live under the illusion that we have *ALL* the information. But no one has all the information. Only God has all the information. We just have *some* of the information.

It seems to me that the people who are making the most trouble in our world are the people who are absolutely sure about everything. It's those who are absolutely sure who become the greatest enemies of peace.

They have told themselves a story. It is a black-and-white story, easy to understand, full of simple solutions to complicated problems. The good guys are the people who are like us, and the bad guys are the people who are not like us.

There is no shortage of arrogant, opinionated people who are absolutely sure about everything. They know just enough to be dangerous, and they are making the world an extremely dangerous place.

On the other hand, it seems to me that the people doing the most good in the world are the people who aren't so sure. They aren't so sure they've got it right. They're pretty certain that there are a lot of things they don't understand. They have some humility wrapped around their opinions.

Proverbs 11:2 says: "When pride comes, then comes disgrace. But with humility comes wisdom."

Humility and wisdom go hand in hand. Certainty and wisdom don't mix so well.

Jesus said: "Blessed are the peacemakers, the meek, those who hunger and thirst after righteousness." He didn't say, "Blessed are those who are certain that they've already achieved righteousness." Instead, He said, "Blessed are those who are *still* seeking righteousness" (emphasis mine), because they're not so sure that they've arrived yet.

> *Humility and wisdom go hand in hand.*

If we're humble about our assessment of the world, we become a lot more willing to shut up and listen. We're a lot more likely to learn something. And we're a lot more likely to be successful as peacemakers.

And, if we're humble about our assessment of the world, we are much less prone to rushing off into something that's going to turn out badly. Because we realize: "You know, I could be wrong."

When pride comes, then comes disgrace, but with humility comes wisdom. And peace, by the way.

We are naturally repelled by arrogance. But arrogance is

so easy to see in others, and so hard to see within ourselves. There is something morally impressive about humble people. We are drawn to them. That's why so many of us have decided to follow Jesus and seek to live by His example and teaching. He is the Prince of Peace. And if we want to represent Him as peacemakers, we must strive to emulate the humility that He has shown.

He is the only one who sees it all. He has the wisdom that can only come from knowing everything about everyone. The wisdom that comes from truly understanding every individual in every culture and location on the planet. He takes into account every circumstance and understands all the variables.

We have to understand that this kind of wisdom can only ever belong to God. His is the only true narrative, the only complete story. He is the only one who's got it all right. Not us. He gets an A+, while we have to settle for an incomplete.

What Good, Small, Faithful Step Can I Take to Encourage Peace?

I can see that my Christian worldview is narrow and that to bring peace, I must seek wisdom and act with humility.

| THREE |

In Defense of Kindness

Many people believe that kindness is for wimps. They believe that meekness is a weakness. But if you think that meekness is a weakness, then try being meek for a week. Kindness and meekness actually require enormous personal strength.

A few years back I was taking my dog for a walk. We live in an area near a river where there is a lot of open space and great opportunities for a dog to explore the world. To get to the big field where she liked to run, we needed to cross one small section of a bike path that cuts through the area. The city regulation is that if you are on the bike path with a dog, that dog must be leashed.

As we were only going to be on the path for 15 yards or so, I didn't feel the need to leash my dog. Call me a scofflaw, but it just seemed silly for such a short crossing. No sooner did we get onto the path than a cyclist came charging up behind us. I mean this guy was flying! As he passed us he yelled in a loud, angry voice, "Hey, put your dog on a leash, idiot!"

Now, up 'til then, I had been in a fine mood that morning. But in a fraction of an instant, my blood was boiling. I yelled out after him: "Hey, it's 10 miles-an-hour speed limit on the greenbelt buddy!" I don't even really know if that's a rule, but I couldn't let his rudeness go unanswered. I had been scolded, yelled at, and disrespected, and I had to come back with something. I had to answer. I had to strike back.

It seems to be hardwired within us…this need to retaliate, to react, to escalate. We don't even have to think about it—so we don't. It's just a reflex. When someone is yelling at us, we yell back.

Here's a little quiz for all you parents: If you are yelling at your child, and your child does not respond as you desire, what do you do? That's simple. You *YELL LOUDER*! It always works so well and is so very effective. Isn't it? Well, maybe not. We all know that yelling louder is a poor strategy for getting our kids to listen to us. So why do we keep doing it?

As human beings, we tend to fall back on these two basic instincts: to yell back, and to yell louder. It hasn't worked to resolve conflicts in the past, it isn't working now, and it's never going to work. Allowing ourselves to get into a shouting war with opponents displays our immaturity and a lack of wisdom. It is always a huge strategic error for anyone who is actually seeking resolution to a conflict.

One of the most important lessons we hope to teach our children is to learn to play well with others. We desire for our children, from their earliest ages, to be with other kids so that they might learn to "play nice." We recognize that these skills are key to their social success and happiness. But it doesn't come easy. Children are selfish little creatures. Conflicts are inevitable.

Consider these 10 Commandments for two-year-olds:

1. If I like it, it's mine.
2. If it's in my hand, it's mine.
3. If I can take it from you, it's mine.
4. If I had it a little while ago, it's mine.
5. If it's mine, it must never, in any way, appear to be yours.
6. If I'm building something, all of the pieces are mine.
7. If it looks *just like* mine, it's mine.
8. If I saw it first, it's mine.
9. If you're playing with something and you put it down, it automatically becomes mine.
10. If it's broken, it's yours.

If we're honest, as adults, we are no better. We are just better at concealing our selfishness. Seeing things from someone else's point of view is a skill that has to be learned.

Knowing how to deal with others when self-interests collide requires maturity, kindness, patience, and restraint. We've all got a lot of growing up to do. People of character are respectful in disputes, and act with civility toward those with whom they disagree.

GOTTA BE RIGHT

To try to describe the *real* obstacle that we face in making peace, let me offer a little hypothetical:

Let's say that you often drive into town with a spouse, a friend, or a co-worker. You disagree about the best route to take. One of you thinks it's best to take the freeway; the other feels it's more efficient to go in by the boulevard. Each of you is convinced that your way is faster, better, more practical. You snipe about this every time you get in the car.

Then, one day, you have to drive in separately. You're leaving at the same time, and going to the same destination, but you each have separate appointments afterward, so you both need a car. Suddenly it occurs to you, *he's going to take the freeway*. And, obviously, you're going to take the boulevard. *Now is your chance to prove you're right!* You *must* get there first!

So it's pedal to the metal. You are screeching tires, weaving in and out of traffic, and generally driving like a maniac. Of course, what you're hoping for is that you get there ahead of him, looking bored and checking your watch. Then you've earned the right to say, "See, I'm right!" Oh, what a glorious moment that will be!

Then you realize that you actually don't really care about the best route to get downtown. You're talking about a difference of one to two minutes, tops. Finding the best route is not actually an issue that concerns you deeply. What really matters to you is that you're right.

In fact, you learn being right matters to you so much that you are willing to endanger your life and the lives of everyone around you just so that you can prove your point. It also means that you are willing to distort the truth in order to appear right. You've distorted the truth by cheating, by driving faster than you normally would. The only real way to know which is the best route would be for both to drive according to the traffic laws. But you're not going to do that because you know that he's speeding, too!

But you don't care. You've just got to be right! You can't concede the point.

And therein lies the chief problem of conflict resolution. We all just so desperately want to be right. What's important to most of us is that *we're not wrong!*

Especially today, people seem so deeply invested in being "right." For so many of us, it isn't about finding solutions, or solving a problem. It's just about winning an argument. This is true in our homes, in our offices, in our neighborhoods, in our national politics, and beyond in our international conflicts.

We have banged on for so long about our opinions that to back down now would make us look weak and foolish. We would appear humiliated and defeated. The truth is the real weaknesses—foolishness, humiliation, and defeat—come when we fail to solve problems and find resolutions.

> *The truth is the real weaknesses—foolishness, humiliation, and defeat—come when we fail to solve problems and find resolutions.*

BEING CORRECT ABOUT POLITICAL CORRECTNESS

If you want to be a peacemaker, then you need to practice kindness. This is especially true when it comes to the way we speak to one another. This doesn't mean letting things go and avoiding all conflict. Real kindness will not be used as a smoke screen for cowardice. Sometimes hard things need to be said. But even hard things can be said with kindness. Genuine kindness is gentle but strong, kind of like a high-quality toilet paper.

These days, you hear a lot of whining and griping about "political correctness." People live in fear of offending some group's "sensibilities" or hurting some person's feelings.

They want to speak plainly, say what's on their mind, call it like it is. They are tired of dancing around while they explain their version of the truth.

On the surface, saying what you want, whatever that is, sounds like a great idea. The danger, however, is that the ones who complain the most about political correctness are often the angriest people. Many of them are fostering a personal agenda far different than what they are describing.

The book of Proverbs is a book of wisdom. It gives this wise advice for anyone who truly wants to be a peacemaker.

A gentle answer turns away wrath,
> but a harsh word stirs up anger. *(Proverbs 15:1)*

As soon as you read that, you know in your heart it's true. You know that it's foolish to be rude, insensitive, harsh, and insulting. The same book also says:

A fool gives full vent to his anger,
> but a wise man keeps himself under control.
> *(Proverbs 29:11)*

Now there's a piece of wisdom for our times, isn't it? How many fools are there out there, giving full vent to their anger? They have lost all desire to exert any self-control in what they say. They think that by offending others they are advancing their cause. In fact, they are the enemies of peace. And, by the way, they are making their case weaker, not stronger. After all, how many people actually listen to the viewpoints of screaming, irrational rioters? It's hard to hear their point of view beyond their actions.

It's almost funny because these very same people are the ones who are most easily offended by what others say. They love the idea of telling how it is, not holding back any punches, and being offensive to others.

But they do not like it when the tables are turned. They do not like it when it is *they* who are offended. They are the first ones to complain loudly when somebody says something about their values or challenge their sensitivities. They can dish out political incorrectness, but they can't take it.

Political incorrectness is like a big sneeze. It feels good coming out, but it leaves snot and a mess everywhere. It has been said, that when you are angry, you'll make the best speech you'll ever regret. So remember the Proverb: *A fool gives full vent to his anger, but a wise man keeps himself under control.*

LEARNING TO PLAY NICE

I used to play pickup basketball with some of my older friends. The games were always fun and friendly. But every now and then, some younger guys would show up at the court, and they would want to argue over every play. They accused somebody of fouling them each time they missed a shot, and the accused would always contest vehemently. Sometimes it would end in shoving and yelling, and it was no fun. Finally, we older guys changed the time that we met, and didn't bother to send the kids the memo. We didn't want to play with them.

So many times I see Christians who are just the same way. They've gotta fight over every point. Someone says something they don't like and they just have to react. Suddenly, there is a flurry of angry emails in my inbox from upset Christians. They are calling "foul." They just can't let it go.

By contrast, when the old guys played together, the most commonly heard phrase on the court was, "Sorry, my bad!" This was partially because we did in fact make a lot of bad plays. But we also said it because it made for a much nicer game. We never called our own fouls. If someone fouled us, we didn't have to protest. Usually the offender would call himself out, "Sorry, I fouled you, my bad." They did this even if they weren't sure they had committed a foul. Sometimes you admit to things even though you're not sure you're at fault. Anybody who's married will understand this. At least anybody who's *still* married.

If you are a grown-up, if you are a mature person, you don't have to win every point. You know that there is virtue and wisdom in letting some things go. So when you hear things from others that don't jive with your view of things, you don't have to react. It's sometimes okay if people think you're wrong when you're not. A mature person can live with that. Because a mature Christian knows that it's not about being right all the time. It's about keeping yourself in the game and playing graciously, so that ultimately, by your example, you can win some to Christ.

Jesus said, "Let he who is without sin throw the first stone." (John 8:7) Of course, no one is without sin. The problem with throwing stones is that eventually everyone gets knocked senseless. That's where we are today. We've been bonking each other in the head for so long that we can't think straight anymore. It's time to stop.

> *A mature Christian knows that it's not about being right all the time.*

We Christians haven't always played well when we've engaged with others who disagree with us. We've been unkind. We need to admit that. Are you without sin? No? Then don't throw stones. Let your words be kind. Your kind words can create the conditions under which peace can thrive.

What Good, Small, Faithful Step Can I Take to Encourage Peace?

I can learn to play nice, realizing that I don't have to be right every single time.

No Forgiveness, No Peace

At the heart of every conflict is some actual or perceived injury. Somebody did somebody wrong or at least we think they did. That somebody is usually somebody else; we never think we are at the source of the problem. But rarely is conflict ever that uncomplicated.

Sure, somebody "started it" (as a five-year-old would say). But most conflicts escalate into a cycle of reprisals, retaliations, retributions, accusations, and insults. It's rare to find a conflict where one party is 100 percent wrong, and the other party is 100 percent right.

Because this is true, peace is never possible until some courageous individual, community, or nation is willing to offer forgiveness, and ask for forgiveness. Somebody started it when it came to the fight, and somebody is going to have to start it when it comes to forgiveness. Do you want to be a peacemaker? Then you've got to be the first one to say you're sorry.

FORGIVE US OUR DEBTS, TRESPASSES, SINS…WHATEVER

Many of us from the Christian tradition grew up saying the Lord's Prayer. You know the one; it goes "Our Father who art in Heaven," etc.

I am the pastor of a nondenominational church. We come from different Christian backgrounds. We do pretty well saying the Lord's Prayer together, especially the first part. We're on the same page with "our Father," "hallowed be thy name," and "give us our daily bread." But the trouble begins when we start the phrase: "forgive us our _____???" Our what? Here we all insert a different word. Some of us say debts, some of us say trespasses, some of us say sins. You say tomato, I say to-mah-to.

It's not just that we're saying different words. We are saying a different number of syllables. It destroys the whole poetry of the thing. At this point in the prayer, the entire recitation becomes a tumbling cacophony.

I'm not sure which denominational group uses which phrase. I had always assumed that the word "trespasses" was used more in your more upscale churches, like the Episcopalians and the Presbyterians. People with money and property worry about trespassing.

But it turns out that "trespasses" is a Catholic word. It seems to me that the word "debt" would be more appropriate for working-class people, like your Catholics, your Methodists, and your Lutherans. Working-class folks worry about debts.

Baptists just call it sin. "Sin" is a good, no-nonsense Baptist word. It has that judgmental quality that you'd expect as a Baptist.

Unitarians don't believe in sin. They say, "Forgive us our occasional foibles, you know we didn't mean it, our intentions were good, we're only human after all."

Debts, trespasses, sins. Whatever you want to call it… "we all done messed up!" All of us! None of us can pretend to be innocent.

All of those words—debts, trespasses, sins—are descriptive. They all add something to the conversation about forgiveness. Trespassing implies that you stepped somewhere you shouldn't have been stepping. You've stepped on someone, or someone has stepped on you.

Failure to pay a debt results in a penalty. You owe someone, you did something, and now you've got to pay. You broke it, you bought it.

Sin. (Now, here's a word with some baggage). We call someone a "sinner" as if some of us are sinners and some of us aren't. But sin just describes the human condition. All have sinned, as the apostle Paul said. God had one thing in mind, and we had another. We chose our way, not God's.

So we pray that our sins will be forgiven. Or our debts, or our trespasses.

But the Lord's Prayer is not the end of it when it comes to forgiveness. The Lord's Prayer is just the beginning. This prayer starts something that only we can finish.

If you study it closely, you'll notice something about the Lord's Prayer. We start out thinking that we are asking God to do things for us, but it turns out that He's asking something from us. And the things He's asking us to do are really hard.

It turns out that we are the ones who have to hallow His name; we are the ones who have to advance His kingdom. It is we who are obligated to carry out His will. Making sure that everyone has his or her daily bread is *our* responsibility.

With the Lord's Prayer, it kind of goes from us asking Him, to Him asking us. And now here comes the hardest "ask" by far. He's asking us to forgive. And maybe harder still, he's asking us to *ask* for forgiveness. Anybody who's ever done either one knows it's about the hardest thing you can ever ask any human being to do.

FATHER, FORGIVE US

We start by asking God to forgive us. Well, that's easy enough. He just waves His magic wand, and it all goes away. He turns the ugly frog into a handsome prince. Yes, Cinderella, you shall go to the ball! All is forgiven. Simple as that.

But we forget the heavy price that was paid for forgiveness. Forgiveness is not easy for God either. In 1 Corinthians we are told, "We were bought at a great price." *(1 Corinthians 6:20)* We are reminded in 1 Peter, "It was not with perishable things such as silver or gold that we were redeemed, but with the blood of Christ." *(1 Peter 1:18)*

Asking God to forgive us must always come with a remembrance of the price. This is not about guilt-tripping. This is about being amazed! That price proves how much He loves us. Remembering the price of forgiveness should fill us with joy and humility.

We ask God to forgive us, because we believe He *wants* to forgive us. We know that He loves us, and we know what He was willing to do for us. We know He'll accept us. The Bible tells us so.

But for most of us, whether it should be or not, the idea of obtaining forgiveness from human beings is much more intimidating. We're pretty sure they don't love us, and we feel certain they don't want to forgive us. We fear that they won't accept us, and we're afraid they won't be at all inclined to forgive us.

GATHER YOUR COURAGE AND ASK FOR FORGIVENESS

You can't really ask for forgiveness from God if you aren't willing to ask for forgiveness from others.

Jesus said, "if you are offering your gift at the altar and there remember that your brother or sister has something against you, leave your gift there in front of the altar. First go and be reconciled to them, then come and offer your gift to God." *(Matthew 5:23)*

> *You can't really ask for forgiveness from God if you aren't willing to ask for forgiveness from others.*

There are three reasons why people don't apologize to those they have wronged. Three reasons why we don't ask for forgiveness. They are the same reasons why communities, tribes, and nations don't ask for forgiveness. They are pride, callousness, or cowardice.

By far, the number one reason that we do not ask others to forgive us is cowardice. We fear that if we bring up our sin, they will release their fury upon us. We fear that they will refuse our apology, unload on us, demand reparations, impose harsh penalties, and dump all of their resentment at our doorstep. Most of the time, these fears prove unfounded.

By the way, they think you don't apologize because you are callous. They think you don't care. They think you're unwilling to acknowledge that you did anything wrong. It's not true, of course. We do care, we know we were wrong, and we are sorry. But the problem is, we're too chicken to admit it.

So gather your courage! Even if it goes badly, you have responded to the call of the Lord's Prayer. In Romans 12:18 the Bible says, "If possible, so far as it depends on you, be at peace with all men. Never mind their reaction, you need to take the initiative and start the forgiveness process. It depends on you."

It's not a concession that the other party is blameless—they probably aren't. But you need to be the one to break the ice, to get the ball rolling, to initiate reconciliation. That's what a peacemaker does.

And when you ask for forgiveness, don't qualify the apology. Don't water it down. Don't say something like, "I'm sorry for what I did, but if you hadn't _____ then I never would have _____." Or "I'm sorry, but I only did that because you _____." Those kinds of statements make for a lame apology.

Any sentence with the word "but" in it is not an apology. In fact, if you put a "but" in your apology, somebody is likely to kick it!

Here's another thing about asking for forgiveness: When I was a kid, I used to get a spanking when I had done something wrong. I usually tried to resist. As I was bent over my mother's knee, I would put a hand behind me to protect the affected area. She would say, "Get that hand down and take your medicine." (Anybody else's mom say that? No? Just mine? Okay, that's why I'm in therapy.)

Here's the point. If you ask someone for forgiveness, and they respond badly and come down on you like a ton of bricks, then get your hand down and take your medicine. You might get spanked, but if you were wrong, you deserve it, so don't try to escape the consequences. If you've hurt someone, you're going to have to face up to the resentment. Just be a big boy or girl, and deal with it.

Proverbs 28 says, "Whoever conceals their sins does not prosper, but the one who confesses and renounces them finds mercy." *(Proverbs 28:13)* And you will find mercy, from God at least, even if not from the one you've injured.

> *There are two things that you can do with blame. You can assign it, or you can accept it.*

There is something else that is so important to understand about asking for forgiveness. This simple concept applies not only to individuals who are in conflict, but also to communities and nations as well. And here it is: Accepting blame for your wrongs makes it safe for others to acknowledge their own failures.

There are two things that you can do with blame. You can assign it, or you can accept it. When you assign blame, you put the other party in a defensive mode. You cause them to put up a wall, to close themselves off from any further dialogue with you. When you accept blame, on the other hand, you disarm your accusers. You soften their attitude toward you. You open the door to helping them understand your perspective.

But assigning blame is so much more common and natural for us. The very first man, Adam, chose to assign blame the moment something went wrong. He said, "The woman you put here with me—she gave me some fruit from the tree, and I ate it." *(Genesis 3:12)* It was the woman, God. The woman and You. You gave me that dreadful woman. You're more at fault that I am.

Can you just imagine the scene with Adam and Eve after they had been expelled from the garden? I would guess Eve said something to the effect of, "What was that back there? Throw me under the bus, will ya? I'd leave you for another man if there was another man."

But what if Adam had "manned-up" and accepted blame? What would Eve have said then? If Adam had said, "My bad, I was wrong, the buck stops here," then I suppose Eve might have said to God, "Hey, it's not all his fault."

If Adam and Eve had both acknowledged their blame, then I wonder what God would have said? I wonder if accepting blame might have kept them in the garden, if it might not have saved mankind. <u>Acceptance of blame makes an environment for healing and forgiveness.</u>

When communities, tribes, and nations are in conflict, there must be courageous leaders who are willing to accept blame for their actions and the actions of their people, or there can be no peace. Peacemakers realize this, and consistently communicate this message whenever they get a chance. And peacemakers lead the way by being the first to acknowledge their own wrongdoing and the wrongdoing of their group. That doesn't mean that the people on the other side of the equation weren't wrong as well. No one is lily-white pure when it comes to conflict. But courageous people who truly desire peace realize that they have to take the initiative and start the process of healing by being the first to ask for forgiveness.

DO YOURSELF A FAVOR AND FORGIVE YOUR DEBTOR

Forgiving someone who has wronged you is really, *really* hard. In some cases, it can be the hardest thing that anybody could ever do. Some of you have been badly injured by others who have purposely damaged you in unimaginable ways. They have ruined your life, they have turned your world upside down. They have left you bleeding and battered, and seem unconcerned with the harm they have left in their wake. How could you possibly ask someone to forgive a person who has acted like that? It's an insult to even suggest it.

Clearly, there are entire populations around the world who feel this way. How can you ask the Jews to forgive the Nazis? How can you ask slaves to forgive slaveholders? How can you ask Syrians to forgive ISIS or Bashar al-Assad? How can you ask Americans to forgive the terrorists who planned and perpetrated the atrocities of 9/11?

Well, I don't know. It's a lot to ask. It angers us even to hear the possibility suggested. It's absurd! But Jesus brings it up. Jesus asks us to forgive. In fact, He demands it of His followers.

But if the offender comes to you and asks for forgiveness, the whole thing becomes a lot easier. If their apology and contrition are genuine and sincere, well, then what can you do? If they are repentant, if they are truly sorry, if they genuinely understand how they were wrong, then I guess we are much more inclined to forgive. It's easier to forgive someone when they ask for forgiveness and when they have shown remorse and genuine repentance.

But usually, the people who have injured us won't ask for forgiveness. They won't ask for the same reasons that you don't ask. Pride, callousness, or cowardice. It's probably cowardice, though I imagine you think it's callousness.

Sometimes, we know they will never ask for forgiveness, because they are not living anymore. They went to their graves with your blood on their hands. They never apologized to you. If people don't ask for our forgiveness, it's much, much harder to give it.

Forgiveness, especially under those circumstances, seems to go against the grain of fairness. It leaves perpetrators unpunished, and it leaves the injured vulnerable to future wrongdoing.

But if you think about it, forgiveness *is* fairness. Without forgiveness, fairness can never be achieved. For the injured party, it comes with a recognition of the need for forgiveness. In the book of Colossians, the apostle Paul said: "Forgive one another just as Christ forgave you." *(Colossians 3:13)* The number one reason to forgive others is because we are all going to need to be cut a little slack ourselves. Forgiveness is fair because we all need it.

But there is another reason why forgiveness is fair. It's fair because it is most helpful to the injured party. Forgiveness bestows its greatest benefit, not to the recipient, but to the giver. If the injured party does not forgive, then it is they who are stuck in prison, not the perpetrator. The injured parties are the ones who are doomed to forever re-live their pain as it replays over and over again in their mind in an incessant loop. Forgiveness releases the forgiver way more than it does the forgiven.

Let's make another thing clear: Vengeance is not fairness. The Bible says that vengeance belongs to God. When we practice revenge, it is like biting a dog because the dog bit us. It is not satisfying, and it leaves you with a nasty, furry-dog flavor in your mouth. In the movies, revenge is always satisfying. But, in real life, revenge leaves you empty, vacant, and hollow.

FORGIVENESS IS A PROCESS

Forgiveness takes time. A lot of people are really disappointed in themselves because they just can't seem to forgive. It's not that they don't want to. They understand that hanging on to past hurts makes them bitter and poisons their soul. Yet their emotions are so strong that they simply cannot get past them.

Forgiveness does not come just because you wish for it, or because you realize it's the right thing to do. Usually forgiveness has to overcome some major barriers. For some, the wounds are very raw, and the injuries very recent. There just has not been enough passage of time for forgiveness to take root. We're going to need more time. God understands.

Others would like to forgive, but it seems impossible because the injury is still ongoing. The offense is not in the past, it's still in the present, and the perpetrator continues to hurt us. The wound can't heal; the scab keeps getting ripped off. It's really difficult to forgive under those circumstances. I suppose some saintly people are capable of it, but most of us aren't. Again, God understands.

You can't fake forgiveness. You can't convince yourself to forgive if your heart isn't there yet. You can't force yourself to forgive someone; you can't talk yourself into it. Many times we think we may have forgiven someone, only to discover later that we haven't.

Forgiveness is a gift from God. In His own time, He gives you the precious gift of being able to forgive another human being who has hurt you deeply. But to receive this gift, you first have to want it. You have to ask for it. You have to be open to forgiveness. You have to desire it. You have to "want to, want to," if you know what I mean.

Please understand: Forgiving is not about forgetting. We hear the phrase, "Forgive and forget." But forgetting is dangerous. It's important to remember. It's important to remember the Holocaust, it's important to remember slavery, it's important to remember the horrors of 9/11.

But it is equally important to avoid being forever stuck in bitterness at the memory of awful events. There is such a thing as redemptive remembering. You remember the events and the wrongs that were done to you. But now you have redeemed your thinking about those things, and realize that those terrible things have shaped you into the person you are today. And those memories are also redeemed by the fact that you survived. You took the hit, and you're still standing. And God used it to bring you to a new place.

In the Old Testament, there is the story of the great patriarch Joseph, whose brothers had sold him into slavery. The wrong that they had done him would be considered by many to be unforgivable. But years later, when Joseph had worked himself into a position of great power, and his brothers, who thought him dead, found themselves begging for his mercy, he said to them, "Do not be afraid. Am I in the place of God? It was not you who sent me here, but God. You intended to harm me, but God intended it for good, to accomplish what is now being done, the saving of many lives." *(Genesis 50:19)*

When we forgive, we save lives. Our own, and many others.

AMAZING GRACE

Following years of apartheid in South Africa, that nation began the healing process by organizing its well-known "Truth and Reconciliation Commission." These proceedings were established to resemble a courtroom in many respects, but it was not an actual court where people were prosecuted, convicted, and sent to prison. This was mostly because it was deemed unwise to send half the country to prison, since the abuses were so widespread. Instead, the commission gave an opportunity for people to tell their stories in a public forum, and for perpetrators to be confronted with the injury they had caused. It wasn't a perfect solution, but it did allow the country to air its dirty laundry and start to move on. And, in fact, some amazing stories did emerge from the proceedings.

One of the most remarkable was a story from a frail black woman, about 70 years old, who rose to testify. Across the room and facing her were several white police officers. One of them was a Mr. Van der Broek, who had just been tried and found culpable in the murders of both the woman's son and her husband some years before. Van der Broek had come to the woman's home, taken her son, shot him at point-blank range and then set the young man's body on fire while he and his officers partied nearby.

Several years later, Van der Broek and his men returned for her husband as well. For months she knew nothing of his whereabouts. Then, almost two years after her husband's disappearance, Van der Broek came back to fetch the woman herself. How well she remembers in vivid detail that evening, going to a place beside a river where she was shown her husband, bound and beaten, lying on a pile of wood. The last words she heard from her husband's lips as the officers poured gasoline over his body and set him aflame were, "Father, forgive them…"

The woman stood in the courtroom and listened to the confession offered by Mr. Van der Broek. A member of the Commission turned to her and asked, "What do you want? How should justice be done to this man who has so brutally destroyed your family?" "I want three things," she said calmly. "I want first to be taken to the place where my husband's body was burned so that I can gather up the dust and give his remains a decent burial." She continued, "My husband and son were my only family. I want, secondly, therefore, for Mr. Van der Broek to become my son. I would like for him to come twice a month to the ghetto and spend a day with me so that I can pour out on him whatever love I still have remaining in me.

"And, finally, I want a third thing. I would like Mr. Van der Broek to know that I offer him my forgiveness because Jesus Christ died to forgive. This was also the wish of my husband. And so, I would kindly ask someone to come to my side and lead me across the courtroom so that I can take Mr. Van der Broek in my arms and embrace him and let him know that he is truly forgiven."

As the court assistants came to lead the elderly woman across the room, Mr. Van der Broek, overwhelmed by what he had just heard, fainted. As he did, those in the courtroom—friends, neighbors, relatives—all victims of decades of oppression and injustice, began to sing "Amazing Grace."

There is nothing in this universe more beautiful than forgiveness. In fact, it's where the whole universe is going. It's the point of all creation. Forgiveness is what this whole story is about. Forgiveness lies at the very heart of God. It's His central plan for history. It's all about amazing Grace.

This is the kind of stuff that changes the world. Peace is never possible until some courageous individual, community, or nation is willing to offer forgiveness, and ask for forgiveness. Blessed are the peacemakers. Do you want to be a peacemaker? Then you've got to be the first one to offer forgiveness.

What Good, Small, Faithful Step Can I Take to Encourage Peace?

When I have hurt someone, I am going to be a courageous big boy or big girl and ask for forgiveness.

FIVE

Peacemaking Is Risky Business

If you watch the news, you know that we live in a scary world right now. Sometimes we long for the good old days…you know, back in 2009 and 2010, when all we had to worry about were the economic meltdown and cooking the planet. Oh, those were simpler times.

Now we have the rise of the Islamic State and other sinister terrorist organizations that make Al-Qaeda look like the Boy Scouts. We have fears about horrible infectious diseases like Ebola and the Zika virus crossing our borders. We have a monumental refugee crisis, which is creating international fear and anxiety as millions are on the move, looking for a safe haven in countries that are already feeling stretched to the limit. It's scary stuff.

Wherever fear rears its ugly head, it complicates peacemaking. In many ways, fear is the worst enemy of peace. Fear makes bad decisions, fear makes us irrational, fear makes us aggressive, and fear makes us hate. Basically, fear makes us stupid, and stupid is never a good omen for peace.

> *In many ways, fear is the worst enemy of peace.*

It's easy, wishful thinking to believe that peace can only be created by diplomats and heads of state. But in a democracy, it is the attitude of average citizens that determine the willingness and ability of political leaders to make compromises and finalize deals. Unfortunately, nothing ties the hands of politicians more than fear among their constituencies.

It is therefore we, the people, whose attitudes and words matter most. And if we, the people, allow our words and attitudes to come from a place of fear and anxiety, then there is little hope for peace in this world.

Opportunity can be found in every crisis. Every act of aggression provides a space for courageous peacemakers to demonstrate mercy, love, and compassion. And when others see those values expressed in real and tangible ways, it has the power to change hearts and minds. Few politicians have the courage to show compassion to people who may represent some risk to their constituents. So it's up to those constituents to lead.

Those average citizens who wish to be peacemakers must tackle the challenge of their own personal fears. Only by looking beyond our fears can we ever hope to envision the courageous solutions that will bring peace. But those fears *are* real, and you've got to know going in…peacemaking is a risky business.

IRRATIONAL FEARS

There are real and personal risks for those who wish to be peacemakers. But life is full of risk. We take them all the time. Some risks are acceptable to us and some are unacceptable. And that is our dilemma. That is what creates the tension, and always makes the actions that would lead to peace so controversial.

It's funny, the risks we're willing to accept. Every day we climb into our cars to go to work, run errands, or take trips. We do this, even though roughly 40,000 people a year die on our roads in this country. That means that since 9/11, over half a million Americans have died as a result of automobile accidents. Driving is risky!

About that same number die every year because they have taken, or have been given, the wrong medications, or have taken them in the wrong amounts.

But we shrug that off. We are not spending trillions of dollars to meet those threats. No politician is talking about protecting *those* American lives. Those risks are not on our radar, though they claim hundreds of thousands more lives than any outside threat.

So why are we so afraid of things that, statistically speaking, represent so little risk? Well, part of the answer is that there are many bad players who intentionally seek to steer us toward irrational fear. Politicians have always found that scaring people is an easy way to manipulate them for political advantage. The cable news industry has discovered that fear and hatred drive their ratings upward. They exaggerate rare and spectacular risks, featuring stories about things that are unlikely to ever happen to you.

When we are being manipulated, we tend to be most afraid of the things that are *least* likely to kill us, and least afraid of the things that are *most* likely to kill us. We don't worry much about the most obvious real and present threat to our lives, which is how we eat. We sit in front of the television, freaked out about Ebola and terrorism, while eating a 16-ounce steak with cheesy fries. Yeah, something's gonna' kill you alright.

The absurdity of it is kinda' funny…except it isn't. More than 600,000 people a year die of cardiovascular disease in the United States, and another 75,000 a year die from complications of diabetes.

Despite the impression that we get watching our hysterical news programming, terrorism is one of the least likely ways that you are going to die. That's just math. It's a horrible way to die, and it's evil, and it needs to be combated. But we at least have to consider the possibility that our fears are overblown, and that those fears are hardening our hearts to good people in desperate need. And that gets in the way of peace.

As I am writing this, there's a great debate going on in our country about whether or not we should allow Syrian refugees to resettle in our cities. The fear is that terrorist organizations will use the opportunity to sneak in some very bad people, to do some very bad things.

This fear has lead some to suggest a ban on all Muslims entering our country. Still others would advocate for a complete and permanent ban on *all* immigration, fearing not only the threat of terrorism, but also the changes that newcomers would bring to our culture. They believe that opening our doors to refugees takes us down a dangerous road. And it does; they're not wrong.

But remember this: All roads are dangerous. There is no such thing as a safe road. Fear is a dangerous road, too. Selfishness is dangerous. It puts our souls in danger. Stereotyping whole populations, or all members of a particular religion, is a deadly, dangerous practice. Thinking that some lives are more valuable than others is a really dangerous road. History has proven that time and time again.

> *Our bodies may be at some risk on one road, but our souls are at risk on the other.*

Our bodies may be at some risk on one road, but our souls are at risk on the other.

AN OPPORTUNITY TO TAKE A RISK FOR PEACE

The current Syrian refugee crisis represents an opportunity to be peacemakers. It represents just one example of how every now and again tragic events conspire to give us a chance to be great.

When Mary was about to give birth to the Prince of Peace, she and Joseph were told there was no room in the inn. They ended up giving birth in a shack out back. That must've been challenging.

You can't help but think of all of the people who turned them away in Bethlehem that night. They missed a huge opportunity. They missed a chance to be great.

If they had only opened the door to Mary and Joseph, we would still be singing about them today. They would be in all our Christmas plays, alongside the shepherds and the wise men. Even the person who let them use a small, smelly stable is now remembered for all eternity. We don't know his or her name, other than "innkeeper," but in all of Bethlehem's history, only King David is more famous.

The people of Bethlehem simply didn't understand who it was knocking on their door. They weren't bad people. The city *was* overcrowded. The young couple had arrived too late. The innkeepers already had a full house. The resources were already stretched thin. The very presence of Mary and Joseph was horribly inconvenient.

The residents of Bethlehem were good people. I'm sure they felt bad about the plight of the couple. But they could legitimately and without guilt turn them away. They had every good reason to do so.

They were good people. But what would great people do?

In the Christmas story, Mary and Joseph are identified with the "outcast and the dispossessed." The Bible informs us again and again that God has a special heart for the outcast, for outsiders, for the stranger, the homeless, the wanderers. Jesus identified with this group throughout His life. This is a major Bible theme. Today, we have no shortage of outcast and dispossessed people in this world. What will our response be to them?

Hard as it was to be homeless that night amidst the stench and filth of the manger, things got worse for the holy family. Herod undertook a campaign to kill all of the male children under two years old. Jesus, of course, was in his "target group." Mary, Joseph, and the child became just one more Middle Eastern family fleeing conflict in the region. They sought refuge in Egypt.

It was a strange country to them. They practiced a different religion. It's easy to imagine that the young family was not well accepted or welcomed. They probably had to rely on the kindness of a compassionate few.

Think for a minute about that word: "Alien." Growing up, if someone had mentioned that word, I would've thought immediately about space aliens. I was raised on a TV diet of *Star Trek* and *Lost in Space*. Those people were always running into aliens. But now, when we hear the word alien, we think of foreigners coming to our country. Aliens and refugees have become a problem for us, and a source of great controversy in our nation.

Did you know that the Bible talks about aliens? There are many references to the word throughout Scripture. Some passages are about how we, as believers, are like aliens in the world. You know: "The world is not my home, I'm just a pass'n through." That kind of thing. These passages tell us that we shouldn't get too attached to the things of this world, because we are ultimately citizens of heaven.

But whenever Scripture talks about foreigners and aliens who are in our land, it encourages kindness and generosity. There's nothing in the Bible about turning away aliens, nothing about leaving them to their fate. Remember this from the Old Testament? "The alien living with you must be treated as one of your native born. Love him as yourself, for you were aliens in Egypt." *(Leviticus 19:34)*

So, why were the ancient Israelites in Egypt? They went there as refugees. They could no longer survive in their own country. There was a famine. They could leave or die. So they went to a more prosperous land desperately hoping to save their families. Any of us would've done the same.

At first they were accepted. But then they became "too numerous," according to the Egyptians. The Egyptian people started to feel threatened and afraid at the growing number of these aliens. They worried that their presence would change the culture, stretch their resources too thin, and impoverish their country. This is how people have always reacted when newcomers come in large numbers to an already established place. These are understandable concerns.

But as the Egyptian's fear grew, their reaction got ugly. They began to look down upon the Hebrew people. They demonized and stereotyped them. They imposed mean-spirited rules on them and forced them to do the hard jobs that no Egyptian wanted to do. Eventually, they enslaved the entire population.

That's why, once the Hebrews had escaped enslavement and returned to their own land, they wrote laws to encourage the compassionate treatment of foreigners and aliens. They were saying, "Remember what it was like to be an alien yourself. Remember what happened to your ancestors. Remember how hard it was for them and how unfairly they were treated. Remember to be better than the Egyptians. Don't act like a jerk toward people who are in a desperate position."

As an American, think for a moment about your immigrant ancestors. They may have been from England or Ireland or Norway or Italy. Most likely they came as economic refugees. They just wanted to save their families.

When they arrived here, it was hard for them. There are always plenty of mean-spirited people in any place and at any point in history. Your ancestors encountered those people. Those already here didn't like their religion, they feared their cultural impact, and they resented that they could not speak the language.

But ultimately, our nation accepted them. And their influence and talents made our country better. The contributions of your immigrant ancestors made America a great country.

Realize this: Every good thing you have, you have because a great country eventually accepted your ancestors. Is America still a great country? Because if it is, it will remember its past and open its heart and doors to reasonable and compassionate refugee policies.

Now, there is no question that things are considerably different today than they were during the great migrations of the 18th and 19th centuries. America is no longer a country of vast open spaces. We are a crowded nation with over 300 million people.

And it is entirely possible, in fact highly probable, that terrorist networks are trying to sneak a few really bad people in among the vast majority of really good people. But clearly, we can't go back to the days of Ellis Island, where they asked your name, checked your teeth, hosed you down, and sent you out into the street.

There are real risks and dangers today associated with accepting refugees. It's not all just paranoia, though there is a good bit of that. Immigrants need to be checked and vetted, and there are no guarantees that someone bad won't slip in between the cracks.

There are risks. But life is full of risk. And by the way, there are very real risks that come with being a fortress nation. I will submit that the risks of closing ourselves off to the world and building walls are significantly greater than the risks and rewards that come when we accept refugees.

We have an opportunity to do something great. To be something great. We have an opportunity to show the world a heart of compassion. To show the Muslim world that we are not what they think we are. Surprise them with our compassion and generosity. We have an opportunity to love our neighbor, and thereby demonstrate the love of Christ.

The refugee crisis is just one opportunity for ordinary citizens to become courageous peacemakers. We have a chance to welcome, assist, and befriend people who are arriving here because their homeland has been torn apart. And it gives us an opportunity to publicly express compassion and support for refugees whenever we encounter fearful and hateful attitudes from our fellow citizens.

These kinds of courageous peacemakers are going to meet a lot of resistance, and encounter people who despise them for their efforts. It's going to take a lot of intestinal fortitude. It's going to take guts. It's going to be hard. There is no sugar-coating that. But it's your chance to be great.

"Peace on earth, goodwill to men!" Is that just a Christmas poem to you, a nice sentiment? Or are you willing to work for it? Are you willing to actually show goodwill to men? Are you willing to help set the tone for peace on earth?

What Good, Small, Faithful Step Can I Take to Encourage Peace?

I can ignore those who spread fear and hatred across my country and instead embrace every challenge as an opportunity to be great.

SIX

Why Being a Prophet for Peace Will Be Unpopular

Let's be honest. People love it when you bark at their enemies. Calling out your enemies involves no risk and requires no courage. It ensures that you are going to be popular with the people on your team. It's a cheap and easy way to win support. It's what politicians do. They play to their base. Give them someone to hate, and they'll love you for it.

But let's get real. Calling out your enemies is cowardice masquerading as courage. It makes you look tough, but it only displays weakness. There is no risk in it, there is no honor in it, and it accomplishes nothing. And, it makes seeking peace much, much harder.

Let me show you what I mean: As a pastor, it would be easy for me to stand up and call out the indiscretions of corporate world leaders. I could blast them for their lack of ethics and morality, for their wrongdoings and shenanigans. But I have no connection to that world. While many in my community might congratulate me on having the guts to "stand up to those people," to me, standing up to "those people" requires no guts. It's easy, and I win points with everyone who is not a corporate executive. From my point of view, there's little to risk, and lots to gain.

But it won't change a thing. My criticisms will roll off their backs like water off a duck.

I'll tell you what would be courageous: It would be courageous if someone from within the corporate community spoke out against corporate practices. <u>Criticism is most effective when it comes from people within your own world and your own culture.</u> The corporate world needs people from within who have the courage to stand up in front of their colleagues, friends, and co-workers and say, "Hey guys, what we are doing is wrong. We can be better than this." And then to watch as their friends stare at them like they're from outer space. Now *that* takes guts—and will ultimately have an impact.

It's corporate executives who need to be calling out corporate executives. It's bankers who need to be calling out bankers. It's union members who need to be calling out unions. It's Republicans who need to be calling out Republicans. It's Democrats who need to be calling out Democrats. And, it's Christians who need to be calling out Christians.

This is the example of the courageous peacemakers of the Bible. This is how you take a real risk. This is how you start moving people away from an "us against them" mentality. This is how you effect change. This is the first step in getting "your people" to make peace with "their people."

Do you want to be a radical peacemaker? Then find the courage to stop sniping at your enemies, and start challenging your friends. Like I said, peacemaking is risky business.

There is a long and venerable tradition of great and courageous people who have advocated for peace, not by hurling insults at those who are natural enemies, but by challenging those who are natural friends. Jesus stood firmly in this tradition. And in so doing, He stood on the shoulders of the Old Testament prophets.

THE PROPHETS OF THE OLD TESTAMENT

I grew up on the San Francisco peninsula, just 20 minutes south of the great city itself. Every Sunday afternoon we drove into the exciting and beautiful City by the Bay. My mom loved it, and I grew to love it, too. We would go to Chinatown, drive down twisty-turny Lombard Street with its beautiful views, and ride the cable cars.

The best part of being in San Francisco was the people watching. It was the late 60s, and we would drive through the Haight-Ashbury region, the center of the hippie movement that was flourishing at the time. It felt like we were driving through a zoo. It was filled with people who seemed wild and strange to us. They were unkempt, with long hair, beards, and crazy eyes. My dad would tell us to keep our windows up. "And, don't feed them!" he would say.

But, by far, the craziest people that you would encounter in San Francisco were not the hippies, but the street preachers. They preached an unhappy and unattractive message of annihilation, destruction, doom, and the end of the world. It wasn't what anybody wanted to hear.

I have a distinct memory of one of these street prophets coming down off his soapbox, walking directly to me, and asking me, "Young man, do you want to go to hell?" I thought to myself, "Buddy, just smelling your breath, I'm already there!"

When we talked about the Old Testament prophets in Sunday School, the San Francisco street preachers were the people I would think of. Crazy, wild scarecrows with long, unkempt hair. They were stern, angry, finger-wagging, scolding old men. And like the words I heard from the street preachers in San Francisco, I wanted to avoid the message of the prophets. I wanted simply to walk to the other side of the street and keep on moving.

The prophets of the Old Testament were not popular while they were living. Just like great artists, prophets are never popular until they're dead. They became heroes after their death. As time passed, everyone agreed that they had been right to speak out against all those bad folks in the olden days. What courage! What wisdom! But if you try to apply any of their teaching to what we are doing in the here and now, well, we don't much like that.

The prophets did not preach to the choir. You know that phrase, right? It means that you say things to your audience that they already agree with or believe in. And, it means you talk right past everybody else. We have a lot of that going on today. Democrats preach to their choir, Republicans preach to theirs. Religious people preach to the religious choir, and secular people preach to the secular choir.

A choir is a great audience; they always applaud. You tell them what's wrong with all the other guys, and tell them why people like us are so great. It's easy to get them all singing from the same song sheet.

Well, the great Israeli prophets did prophesy against other nations from time to time. But most of the time, the great Israeli prophets prophesied against the Israelites. And, the Israelites didn't like it one little bit. Isaiah was sawn in half, Amos was beaten with a club, Habakkuk was stoned to death in Jerusalem, Jeremiah was stoned to death in Egypt.

Years later the Israelites saw that the prophets were right and that the people should've listened. Too late, they made the prophets great men and cherished their words. Of course, it's easy to see that in hindsight.

Jesus didn't preach to the choir either. He challenged the people that should've been on His "team," so to speak.

He warned them about the tendency to honor the dead prophets, and hate the living ones. He said, "Woe to you, teachers of the law and Pharisees, you hypocrites! You build tombs for the prophets and decorate the graves of the righteous. And you say, 'If we had lived in the days of our ancestors, we would not have taken part with them in shedding the blood of the prophets.' So you testify against yourselves that you are the descendants of those who murdered the prophets." *(Matthew 23:13)*

Jesus made it clear to them that they were carrying on the heritage of the executioners. He was thinking that they thought just like them. They carried the exact same mentality. And they too would end up on the wrong side of history.

It's so easy to look back in history and say things like, "If I had lived in the 1850s, I would have opposed slavery." But look at the way you think about things now, and tell me you would've opposed slavery. Are you sure?

The abolitionists were hated by the rest of the Christian community. They were the radicals, the crazy people, completely out of their minds! Everyone said to just ignore them, they're nuts.

Well, it's easy to see who was right and who was wrong as we look back in history. But it's hard to listen to the visionaries when the right thing threatens your way of life today.

The great historical lesson of the prophets, and of Jesus'

teaching as well, is that we need to pay attention to the people who make us mad. Because they just might be right. And we need to be willing to anger our friends if we want to be peacemakers. It's a big risk to take. You might even get crucified.

PEACEMAKERS WILL LOVE THEIR ENEMIES AND CHALLENGE THEIR FRIENDS

Did you ever make the wrong person mad? Maybe someone in your own family, or possibly your boss? Maybe it was someone even scarier…the president of your local homeowners association? Someone who has power over you? Someone who can reward or punish you? Someone who can make your life miserable?

You don't necessarily have to do something stupid to make people mad. Sometimes you simply can make people mad by doing something great. Here is a great truth of history: Good people stay out of trouble. But great people are in trouble all the time.

Jesus got into hot water with the wrong people. The irony is that these are the people who could have been His natural allies.

Jesus could have found a natural ally with the Zealots. We think of a zealot as someone who is obsessed, driven, or crazy. They've developed an overwhelming loyalty to an idea or a cause, to the point of annoyance for everyone around them. But in Jesus' time, "Zealot" was the name given to a Jewish religious and political party centered in Jerusalem. This was an underground group, an illegal, outlawed political organization. If the Romans knew you were a Zealot, you would be crucified. So they got very good at hiding their affiliation. It was a secret organization, but a big organization, with many active members, and even more sympathizers.

The Zealots wanted to establish the Kingdom of God. Jesus had exactly the same goal! They were on the same team. Jesus could have found a natural ally in the Zealots.

But instead, He seemed to go out of His way to make them angry. They thought they could establish the Kingdom of God by taking the land back by force. But Jesus would have none of that. Instead, He befriended and showed kindness to the natural enemy…the Roman soldiers.

We see an example of this in Matthew 8. Here Jesus speaks to the enemy, a Roman centurion—in fact, a leader among the occupying forces. Just speaking to such a man was enough to enrage a Zealot. But beyond that, He heals His enemy's servant! Talk about giving aid and comfort to the enemy!

Most infuriating of all, Jesus actually commended the faith of this occupier. He said of the centurion, "I tell you the truth, I have not found anyone in Israel with such great faith." *(Matthew 8:10)* This would be a highly offensive statement to a Zealot. This centurion was an agent of the devil. Why even speak to him? And, to suggest that he had greater faith than anyone in Israel was outrageous. This man was an out-and-out pagan. It was the Zealots who should be commended for their faith. They had so much faith they were willing to kill and die for the Kingdom. How dare Jesus claim that this pagan, this mercenary, this oppressor, this murderer, had more faith than they did?

In another instance, one of Jesus' most famous sayings was intended as a direct slap in the face of the Zealots. Jesus said: "I tell you, do not resist an evil person, but if someone strikes you on the right cheek, turn to him the other also." *(Matthew 5:39)*

When we hear this passage today, we think about some rude guy at work, or a conflict in your family, or maybe a mean neighbor across the street. But when Jesus spoke about enemies, whom do you suppose everyone was thinking about? They were thinking about the Romans, the occupying force. Jesus was speaking directly to the Zealots, and He was talking about rejecting the political violence that they advocated. He continued, "And if someone wants to sue you and take your tunic, let him have your cloak as well, if someone forces you to go one mile, go with him two miles." *(Matthew 5:41)*

This was specifically about Roman soldiers, who had

the legal authority to demand food or shelter, and who could, by law, force someone to carry their gear for up to one mile. Imagine how much anyone would resent that. Can you imagine if we had been occupied by the Russians back in the days of the Cold War and then were encouraged to be nice to the occupiers? Could there be a more unpopular message? Especially for a Zealot?

Another direct shot at the Zealots is seen in the Sermon on the Mount. Jesus said, "Blessed are the peacemakers, for they will be called sons of God." *(Matthew 5:9)* In other words…the Zealots were not the sons of God. You do not represent God by blasting your enemies. But you do make peace when you challenge your friends.

Today, so many Christians believe that they advance the Kingdom of God by blasting their enemies. I am constantly being invited to attend seminars and conferences about the dangers and evils of Islam. Anti-Muslim sentiment and rhetoric is at an all-time high among Christians.

But talking smack about other religions does not hallow His name or hasten the coming of His kingdom. When we put down other religions, it always makes us look small, petty, paranoid, and delusional. As Christians we've got enough flaws and failings of our own, and we don't need to be diverted by talking about what's wrong with everybody else. Once we get ourselves in order, then maybe we can start in on the other religions. What was that stuff Jesus said? Something about he who is without sin being able to throw the first stone? Something about taking the 2x4 out of your own eye before you start worrying about the sliver in the other guy's eye?

When we denigrate and disrespect other religions, we dishonor the name of God and put the brakes on His kingdom coming. The Zealots were wrong. We don't get to peace by making war on our enemies. We get to peace by challenging our friends.

SPEAK UP FOR YOUR ENEMIES

All this "love your enemies" business is pretty hard to swallow. But Jesus consistently encouraged love for enemies. And He consistently alienated people who could have been His natural allies.

> *Our mission is to make disciples, not to alienate potential disciples.*

So many people today believe that the mission of the church is to make the world safe for Christians. They have turned Christianity into a Christian rights movement. Their primary focus is to protect and defend Christians, eliminate all outside threats, and drown out the voices of all secular and religious enemies.

But this attitude could not be farther from the attitude

of Christ. Jesus is clear about our mission. Our mission is to make disciples, not to alienate potential disciples. The goal is not to avoid persecution. The mission is to hallow the name of God and to hasten the coming of His kingdom. Our mission is not to make the world safe for Christians.

He told us we should absolutely expect to be persecuted. We are quite clearly told by Jesus that hallowing His name and hastening the kingdom will be a dangerous job, and we should know going in that we will be persecuted. Count on it!

In fact, in many places around the world, we know Christians are being persecuted and even killed. We should absolutely advocate for them and seek justice on their behalf. But why is it that Christians only ever seem to advocate for other Christians, and do not speak up for others who are persecuted around the world? How is that Christlike?

Jesus said, "If you only love those who love you, what credit is that to you? Even the pagans do that." *(Matthew 5:46)*

There are a lot of persecuted people in this world. They are disrespected, imprisoned, beaten, separated from their families, starved, and often killed. They are people who do not deserve what is happening to them.

And many of them, in fact most of them, are not Americans, and they are not Christians. But they matter to God, too.

If we're going to fight for liberty and justice, then let's fight for liberty and justice for all...not just for our tribe members. Not just the American, but the Iranian, too. Not just the Christian, but the Muslim as well. Not just for white people, but for the African-American and for the Hispanic and for the Arab.

If we only fight for our rights and the rights of people like us, that just makes us like everybody else. It makes us small, petty, and tribal. And no one is going to want to join that tribe.

When we make Christianity a Christian rights movement, we disrespect the name of God and slow the Kingdom's progress. But if we speak up for our enemies, and champion the rights of those people outside of our tribe, we honor Christ, we hasten the coming of His kingdom, and we hallow His name.

Remember what Jesus said in the Beatitudes in Matthew 5.

Jesus also said, "Let your light shine before men in such a way that they might see your good works and glorify your father who is in heaven." *(Matthew 5:16)*

It does not say, "Let your sensibilities be offended in such a way that men might see your outrage and glorify your Father who is in heaven." Or, "Let your anger burn in such a way that men might see your hatred and glorify your Father who is in heaven."

One of the best ways to do that is to love and defend your enemies. I'm afraid it will make your friends very unhappy. But it is an essential first step down the road to peace.

What Good, Small, Faithful Step Can I Take to Encourage Peace?

I will not talk smack about other religions or nationalities, knowing that Jesus has called us to love *all* people.

The Other Side of the Road: Racial Attitudes and Peacemaking

When I was a little kid in Sunday School, we used to sing a song...

Jesus loves the little children, all the children of the world.
Red and yellow, black and white,
They're all precious in His sight.
Jesus loves the little children of the world.

Of course, in my Sunday School class there were no red or yellow or black children. But we were quite sure that He loved them wherever they were.

Now that I'm older, I realize that the remarkable thing is not that Jesus loves the little children...little children are easy to love. The truly amazing fact is that He also loves the stubborn, bickering, hostile, and prejudiced adults.

Most of us have been to Disneyland and gone on the "It's a Small World" ride. This attraction features mechanical children from all over the world singing, *"It's a small world after all,"* and now that I have mentioned it, you will have that song stuck in your head for the rest of the day. But what would happen if it weren't children featured on that ride, but adults? What if Tinker Bell sprinkled her magic fairy dust, and all the mechanical children became grown-ups? Suddenly, it would become Pirates of the Caribbean. They'd all be shooting at each other and end up burning the place down.

The fact is that there is something about adults…when they find the least little difference between one another, they gather into little teams and tribes made up of people exactly like themselves. They talk up the things that are great about their little clan, and discuss how terrible everyone else is. What is it with us, that even here in the 21st century, we can't embrace the simple concept of a small world where differences are to be celebrated instead of feared? We've come this far through human history and still see widespread racial hatred and violence, resulting in war and injustice around the world. It

> *It seems that the only thing we have learned from history is that we don't learn from history.*

seems that the only thing we have learned from history is that we don't learn from history.

It has always been true, from the very beginning of time, that racial tension has been at the center of conflict and violence. So many of our wars, past and present, have ultimately been about racial hatred. We don't have to think very hard to recall these events. The Jewish Holocaust, the genocide in Rwanda, the conflict between Israelis and Palestinians, apartheid in South Africa, the Balkan wars. And these are just recent examples from within the last hundred years. Religion often gets the credit for instigating most of history's wars. But the truth is that race is most often at the center of human conflict, and people use their religion to justify their racial hatred.

Many people are surprised to discover that Jesus had something to say about race. He spoke to the problem directly in a story that we don't usually associate with the issue. We think of His famous story of the Good Samaritan *(Luke 10:25-37)* as a story about helping those in need. Of course, it is about that, and that is an important part of the parable. But Jesus made the hero of the story a Samaritan, and in so doing, He made a powerful statement against racism. He told the story in response to a question: "Who is my neighbor?" It wasn't a new question. For centuries Jewish scholars had debated it. The question had arisen from a statement in the Torah: "Love your neighbor as yourself."

(*Leviticus 19:18*) Many wanted to define a "neighbor" as a fellow Hebrew, someone who looked as they did, spoke as they did, shared the same history. They did not want to consider people who were different from them as neighbors... people like the Arabs who surrounded them, or especially people like the Samaritans.

Samaritans were considered by Jews to be half-breeds: half Jewish and half Arab. Many Jewish people felt that Samaritans had corrupted the Jewish religion. They looked down on Samaritans, had derogatory names for them, treated them as second-class citizens, segregated them from Jewish society, and considered them unclean. In the year 9 CE, when Jesus would have been a little child, a group of frustrated Samaritans scattered human bones around the Temple in Jerusalem (Josephus *Antiquities,* 11.342-346). This was incredibly offensive to the Jewish people...a really bad Halloween prank. When Jesus spoke this parable, tensions between Jews and Samaritans were sky high. You can be sure that making a Samaritan the hero in His story was no casual or random choice. Jesus was making a statement about race, and that's why this story was told.

We all know the tale...a man was walking on a very dangerous road and overcome by robbers who beat him and left him for dead. Soon afterwards, a couple of religious guys came down that road, saw the man, and passed by on the other side to avoid helping him. Finally, another man came, the man you would least expect to help the unfortunate Jewish traveler…a Samaritan.

If we think about the different people in this story, we can see that they fall into three categories. The first category is the robbers whose attitude was, *"What's Yours Is Mine—I'll Take It."* The second category is the religious characters, the priest and the Levite, whose attitude was, *"What's Mine Is Mine—I'll Keep It."* The third is the Samaritan, whose attitude was, *"What's Mine Is Yours—I'll Share It."* When it comes to race relations throughout history, and around the world today, we can still see the same attitudes at work.

WHAT'S YOURS IS MINE—I'LL TAKE IT

The bandits on the road displayed the classic criminal mindset: *"What's Yours Is Mine—I'll Take It."* Criminals say, "I don't care if it belongs to you…I want it…I'm going to take it… without your permission, and regardless of the consequences to you." This is the criminal mentality, the mentality of robbers, thieves, and three-year-olds. We all recognize it as selfish and wrong. And yet, it has not only been criminals who have held this view of the world. Sometimes it has been governments or ethnic groups that have displayed this same attitude.

At times in history, the church itself has condoned and endorsed this attitude toward racial populations that it considered inferior. In the 16th, 17th, 18th, 19th, and well into the 20th century, leaders of the great nations of Europe traveled all over the globe, to every continent, conquering and subjugating lands and their peoples, and carrying along with them this attitude: What's yours is mine—I'll take it. They took the diamonds, they took the silver, they took the gold, and they took the agricultural resources. They stole away their autonomy, they drew lines on a map to divide things up in a way that would be economically convenient for them but resulted in disaster for the people who lived there. Worst of all, they stole the very lives and identities of human beings, enslaving them for their own profit. This is perhaps the ultimate expression of the mentality, "What's yours is mine—I'll take it."

I guess it's easy for me to talk…that was a long time ago, and I wasn't there. The fact is that if I had been born during that time, I probably would have carried within me the same attitude, would have committed the same sins. Had I been there, I might have…but I wasn't, and I didn't. I'm not guilty! I never held slaves or confiscated property that didn't belong to me. I don't carry the "what's yours is mine" mentality. But I might be guilty of something else.

WHAT'S MINE IS MINE—I'LL KEEP IT

The second attitude is that of the religious men, the priest and the Levite, who walked by on the other side of the road.

Their thinking was, "What's mine is mine—I'll keep it." Growing up we thought, "These guys are terrible, these are the real antagonists of the story." They could've helped and didn't…what's wrong with these people?

But there may have been some good reasons why they didn't stop to assist the victim. On this particular road, it was a common trick for bandits to plant a decoy just like this…someone pretending to be hurt. When the poor bleeding-heart sap came over to help, they would jump him and leave him robbed and bloody. This road was notoriously dangerous, and smart people were careful and guarded when they traveled on it.

It is also possible that as these men walked down this road, they weren't merely thinking of their own personal interests in avoiding the injured party. Maybe they were thinking, "Hey, I've got a family back home, and they depend on me, they count on me coming home safely." They had people to take care of, and felt it would not be prudent; it would not be responsible for them to put themselves at risk like that. There were no life insurance policies, and widows were often left in a dire circumstance.

Another legitimate thought that they may have had was, "How many beaten and bloody guys am I going to find along this road? This is a long road and filled with people who have problems. I simply don't have the time or resources to take care of everyone on this road; it is simply too much."

As we consider these factors, we may come to the conclusion that they were acting reasonably…they held a reasonable point of view. We feel the same way ourselves. We have a responsibility to our family. We know that there are people who will try to deceive and take advantage of us. And, we certainly can't meet every need that we are presented with. "What's mine is mine—I'll keep it" makes a certain kind of sense…it is a reasonable point of view.

But, there is a problem with it. It is not the point of view to which Jesus is calling us. If we are serious about being His disciples, if we desire to be His followers, if we are committed to His lordship in our lives and to furthering peace in our world, then we cannot carry the kind of attitude that says, "What's mine is mine—I'll keep it."

So many of the conflicts in our world occur because people hold this point of view. People feel threatened by others who they believe are going to take away some of what is theirs. And most of the time, those are people who belong to another racial group. We don't want them moving in on our territory, drawing down our resources, cutting into our piece of the pie. And race is of course the easiest way to define the threat. It's the easiest, most clear-cut dividing line between "us" and "them." It becomes easy to blame "them" for threatening our way of life and our standard of living.

CLEANING UP THE MESS

When my kids were living at home, I would sometimes come downstairs and there would be this big mess in the kitchen or living room. I would call to them and say, "You kids get in here…who made this mess and left it?" The remarkable thing was that nobody made the mess! No one would own up. I was left to assume that evil fairies lived in our home and made messes while we slept. I told the kids, "Alright, even though none of us made the mess, we are all going to clean it up together, because we are a family and we all live here together." Can you guess what their response was to that? "THAT'S NOT FAIR!!! Why should we have to clean up a mess that we didn't make? It's not my mess!"

Well, our ancestors made a mess. And, they're not going to clean it up…they're all dead. And so, because we live in this place together, this place called the United States of America…and because we are a family…we have to be the ones to clean it up. This is what Jesus is telling us in this story, that we have to move beyond the "what's mine is mine" mentality. We have to move beyond that to something better, to the third attitude demonstrated in this story.

WHAT'S MINE IS YOURS—I'LL SHARE IT

The Good Samaritan carried the viewpoint that held, "What's mine is yours—I'll share it."

> A Samaritan, as he traveled, came where the man was; and when he saw him, he took pity on him. He went to him and bandaged his wounds, pouring on oil and wine. Then he put the man on his own donkey, took him to an inn and took care of him. The next day he took out two silver coins and gave them to the innkeeper. "Look after him," he said, "and when I return, I will reimburse you for any extra expense you may have. *(Luke 10:33-35)*

What's mine is yours—I'll share it.

What Jesus is telling us here is that it is not enough to say, "Hey, I'm not a racist! I believe in diversity and I believe in racial tolerance and equality, and I don't mind hanging out with people of color on occasion." Jesus is saying that is not good enough. He is expressing that we need to do more than that; we need to do more than decency requires. We need to go the extra mile, we need to take the risks, we need to cross the lines, we need to go to the other side of the road. We need to go to that side of the road where people have been beaten and injured and robbed by those who acted with a criminal mentality. We need to clean up their mess.

We all know the old joke about why the chicken crossed the road. There are many interesting variations to be found on the Internet:

The New York City police said, "You give me five minutes with da chicken and I'll find out."

Hemingway said, "He crossed the road. To die. In the rain."

Martin Luther King, Jr. said, "I see a world where all chickens will be free to cross roads, and thank God a-mighty, be free at last."

Bill Clinton said, "To the best of my recollection, that chicken did not engage in what I would call 'road crossing behavior.'"

So here's the question for us today: Why does the Christian cross the road? The answer is that he crosses the road to follow Jesus. She crosses the road to clean up the mess that somebody else has made. This is why churches must provide as many opportunities as they can for their people to cross the road. This is why Christian organizations are taking millions of American Christians to Africa and to South America on mission trips, to literally cross the road, or the border, or the ocean, in a desire to follow Jesus and make a dent in cleaning up the mess. This is why there is a new emphasis on integrating our churches and starting multicultural congregations, so that we don't just occasionally hang out with people who are different, but instead actually live in community with people who are different. This is why we must partner with those organizations that seek to develop entrepreneurship in the underdeveloped regions and neighborhoods of our country, and break old cycles of dependency by giving real opportunity. This is why churches should be taking the lead in integrating refugees into their communities. These ways, and many others, are how we get ourselves to the other side of the road and clean up that old mess. We are His followers, and that means that we must be His leaders.

How will you cross the road? What will you do to clean up the mess? Because really, what's yours is His…what's yours was never really yours to begin with. His desire is that we share the resources He has so freely given with our neighbors.

GOING OUT OF OUR WAY

Look, a lot of people are talking about race and conflict. A lot of conversation is taking place, especially right now on the national level. The deaths of so many black men at the hands of white police officers, and the subsequent hatred and violence directed towards law enforcement, have brought the issue front and center in the American consciousness.

Much of the conversation is helpful and positive. A lot of people are saying a lot of good things about how we can move forward, how we can be better. While some people become harder, more militant, more stubborn, and more prejudiced, many more people are awakening to their own personal biases and false assumptions. The high-profile racial encounters, so often caught now on cell phone video, are making us take a harder look at the truth about race in our country.

But all the words, and all the good ideas are not really going to change anything. Things will only ever change when enough of us make it a priority to go to the other side, to build friendships and long-lasting relationships with people who have a different racial makeup than we do. We have to go out of our way to do this. Society does not make it easy, and there are many cultural barriers. It may not be the most comfortable thing, but it *has* to happen.

These kinds of friendships will only be built by people who are willing to endure the discomfort and get to know people as people. Over time, these relationships will help us to understand a different point of view and feel a connection instead of a threat. Real peacemakers will see this as an essential part of their mission. We have to literally go out of our way to do this. Nothing about it is convenient or easy. But it's the only way we're ever going to experience racial peace.

Jesus loves the little children; red and yellow, black and white, they're all precious in His sight. They can become precious in our sight, too, and their parents' as well. But only if we'll follow His lead and go to the other side of the road.

What Good, Small, Faithful Step Can I Take to Encourage Peace?

I will cross the road and go out of my way to make peace by making friends and establishing ongoing relationships with people who have a different racial make-up than I do.

EIGHT

Making It Happen—Practical Steps Toward Radicalizing Peace

So far this book has been about the kinds of attitudes, thoughts, perspectives, and words that are characteristic of a true peacemaker. These are the essential building blocks for peace, and communicating these points of view is the greatest thing we can do to lay the groundwork for peace in our neighborhoods, tribes, communities, and world.

But, in addition to this, there are other very practical steps that we can take to work for peace. In this chapter we are going to highlight some of those steps.

Of course, there are many peacemakers who have dedicated their entire lives, or at least a major chunk of their lives, to the pursuit of peace. You might be inspired to do the same, as there are many career avenues to pursue, as well as shorter-term possibilities for extended volunteer work.

We are grateful for the many civil servants who choose to become career diplomats. They work in the State Department or at the UN. They are professional peacemakers whose service is worthy of honor and respect. They work long hours under difficult conditions where there are no easy solutions. It's their job to be peacemakers, and they spend all of their waking hours concentrated on the effort.

Countless numbers of peacemakers have decided to go to work for nonprofit agencies whose mission is to foster peace. They, too, work long, tireless hours, usually for little pay. They work for organizations like Bread for the World, the Carter Center, Save the Children, International Justice Mission, and so many others.

In addition to this army of full-time workers, increasing numbers are choosing to dedicate months or years of their life to volunteering their energies for just a season. Throughout its history, more than 200,000 Americans have served with the Peace Corps to promote a better understanding between Americans and the people of 139 host countries. Today, 8,655 volunteers are working with local communities in 77 host countries. Doctors Without Borders has commanded the respect and admiration of millions as they have inspired volunteer physicians, nurses, and other healthcare workers to travel to some the world's most difficult and dangerous places.

But, the truth is, most who are reading this book are

probably not able to pursue peacemaking careers or donate major portions of our lives to volunteer in faraway places. We are working people, with the kinds of obligations and responsibilities that include kids, mortgages, locked-in careers, and connections in our community, and we are not likely to pull up roots and run off to Timbuktu.

So what can we do? If you're just a regular gal or guy who wants to make a difference, how can you get involved? Here are some suggestions. There's nothing profound here, just a few ideas to jumpstart your own personal exploration in more depth.

1. START A SMALL HOME BOOK OR STUDY GROUP FOCUSED ON PEACE

If you've never been a part of a small-group community, then you really don't know what you're missing. Whether it's a Bible study or a book club or a quilting bee, small groups of people who gather together regularly develop a sense of friendship and community that is hard to find in today's world. It enriches your life and connects you with other human beings.

So why not think about starting a small group focused on educating yourselves about peace? Think about the friends you have and the people you know who might be interested in the subject. It might be something you promote in your church, or you may even connect with people on Craigslist!

There are many curriculum resources available for those who would like to start a group like this. For example, great group discussion materials are available from

1) *Carter Center* (http://www.cartercenter.org/news/teacher_resource/latest.html)
2) *International Justice Mission* (http://institute.ijm.org/?_ga=1.86871960.1484918276.1465573127)
3) *Saddleback Church* (http://saddleback.com/archive/blog/small-groups-blog/2008/12/25/small-group-curriculum-the-peacemaker?contentid=1717)
4) *Brethren Press (*http://www.brethrenpress.com/SearchResults.asp?Search=enemylove&Search.x=0&Search.y=0)

These are just a few examples that can easily be found through the website of your favorite group or through a quick Google search.

By far the most in-depth and academically challenging collection of peace-related material that we could find comes from an organization called START...an acronym for "study, think, act, respond together" (http://www.start-guide.org). The website provides guidance on how to pull a group together, modify the process to meet your needs, and run a group. The START reading list links directly to the material, which is all free and accessible online.

Another idea for your group is to invite a guest speaker, maybe a former Peace Corps volunteer living in your town, or someone who has been active in an organization that promotes peace. Christian Peacemaker Teams is one group that will provide speakers for this purpose. You can connect with them at http://www.cpt.org/participate/speaker.

Whatever you choose to study or read, you are sure to stimulate ideas and direct action steps that you can take together to make a profound impact.

2. DONATE TO A PEACEMAKING GROUP THAT YOU BELIEVE IN AND TRUST

One thing you can probably guess…organizations that work hard for peace are not generally swimming in cash. It's not easy to have major impact without major money. But somehow most of these organizations are figuring out a way to get a lot done with minimal resources.

I hope that all of you have discovered the joy that comes in giving away some of your money to organizations and causes that you truly believe in. There's an old saying that you've probably heard: "Money talks." This is true. In my case, money talks all the time. Mostly it says "goodbye."

There's another old saying: "Money can't buy happiness." I want to suggest to you that *that* is wrong. Money *can* buy happiness. It's just that we're spending our money the wrong way. Research consistently shows that generous people are more happy. So how can you enjoy life more and like yourself better? That's easy. Be boldly generous.

Sit down and figure out a way to give a healthy and sacrificial percentage of your income to those organizations that are making a difference for peace in our world and in our communities. But we need to be smart about this, right?

There is no question that some organizations use money more wisely, effectively, and efficiently than others. There are several websites that rank charities based on a variety of criteria designed to measure effectiveness and trustworthiness. Charity Navigator is one of these. They can be found at http://www.charitynavigator.org. They have provided a list of charities with the most consecutive four-star ratings. Among the peace organizations that are included in their list are Compassion International, the Children's Aid Society, Kids Alive International, Institute for Justice, MAP International, and Save the Children.

There are of course other lists of top-rated charities from other monitoring organizations. My suggestion is that you take a close look at where your favorite organization stands and how it measures up against the criteria for excellence in the areas of finance, accountability, transparency, and effectiveness. You definitely want to direct your giving in a way that "gives peace a chance."

3. LOBBY YOUR LEGISLATORS

For a lot of us, lobbying is a dirty word. We think of lobbyists as scheming individuals who make enormous amounts of money by corrupting our system and representing special interests at the expense of the common good. We are disgusted by the whole idea of lobbying.

It's true enough that our current system of lobbying has made money "king" among politicians and undermined our democracy, giving a small number of mega-corporations and special interests a disproportional influence at the expense of other voices.

But it is also true that any private individual can lobby his legislators and become a squeaky wheel, a voice of conscience, or a thorn in a side. They also can provide valuable educational interactions for any legislator, getting them to see something that they might have missed or to better appreciate a different point of view. Individuals and small volunteer associations are doing this all the time, and they are having a real effect. These grassroots volunteer lobbyists are unpaid and operate without the firepower that the big boys have. But they can and do make a difference.

Where to start? To begin with, you can make contact

with your legislators, be they city council members, commissioners, congressmen, or senators. With a little Internet research, you'll find a way to reach them by email. Nearly always, they will have a webpage that gives an email address or provides an opportunity for you to comment directly on the site. Even a good old-fashioned letter can still find its way to their inbox. Some argue that that is even more effective, particularly if it is handwritten, because it stands out in an age when everyone is overwhelmed by email and other digital bombardments.

Clearly these letter-writing or email campaigns are much more effective if the number and volume of communications received are higher. There is definitely power in numbers. You can write two or three times a week, but it is even more effective if you organize a group of volunteer letter-writers. The more the better, obviously. You might connect with organizations who share your values and ask if they have letter-writing campaigns, and if not, if you could organize one that would encourage their members to participate. They are sure to be enthusiastic about your efforts.

There are many sample letters that you can find online that provide a template for effective communication with a legislator. You will want to write a letter that is respectful and kind and avoid engaging in an angry tirade. People always respond better when they are treated with respect. And yes, politicians are people, too.

In the same vein, you can also leave phone messages. You can call your national senator or congressman by dialing 1-202-224-3121 and asking the Capitol switchboard for your member by name. Most likely you will only be able to leave a message or possibly talk with a staffer. But always ask to speak with the representatives themselves. If you call often enough, one day they just may get on the line with you. But, as with writing letters, you'll want to maintain a respectful tone at all times, and again there are scripts available online to help you keep on point. And, as with writing letters, your message is much more impactful if it comes as a part of a larger campaign that overwhelms the representative's office with calls.

> *You can call your national senator or congressman by dialing 1-202-224-3121 and asking the Capitol switchboard for your member by name.*

You also can ask to make an appointment to meet with your representative personally. Clearly, this becomes more difficult as you move up the chain. You are unlikely to get an appointment with the President of United States. I mean, go for it for sure, but don't hold your breath. On the other hand, you are very likely to have a chance at a meeting with the state representative from your local district. You might be able to arrange an appointment through the office, or you might meet them at a public event and have a brief opportunity to speak. It may be that the best you can do is to get a meeting with a member of their staff. That's still good, and probably more effective than just writing a letter or leaving a message. Persistence is the key here. Don't give up just because you've been put off a time or two…or three or four.

And, again, remember…be nice! Be charming! Listen as well as speak. Bring a sense of humor along with you. You're supposed to be a peacemaker, right? Help them to see your point of view by being reasonable and kind. Represent your cause well, and be an ambassador of the Prince of Peace.

4. PARTICIPATE IN PEACEFUL PROTESTS

For as long as human societies have existed, people have been organizing protests. The ancient Israelites protested against Moses for leading them out of slavery in Egypt, only to die in the desert, which still sounds better to me than slavery. Then again, I wasn't there.

Protesting has a mixed history. At times, it has changed the world dramatically. We think of the collapse of the Soviet Union, where men like Vaclav Havel and Lech Walesa organized protests that brought a major world power to its knees.

We think, too, of the civil rights protests in our own

country during the 1960s. We think of sit-ins and boycotts and bus tours and marches. Some of those images are burnt deep into our national consciousness, and we honor them as the wake-up calls that brought major shifts in public opinion. We think of the march on Washington in 1963 that packed the square in front of the Lincoln Memorial, filled with over 250,000 civil rights supporters, as Dr. Martin Luther King delivered his famous speech. Yeah...protests can make a difference.

But when we think of protests, we also think of riots and looting and arson and ugliness. We think of anger and hatred and violence, and counter-protesters clashing in the streets. We associate protesting with extremists and radicals. We sense that maybe protesting only hardens the positions of those who are for and those who are against. It feels like it divides us way more than it unites us.

We also see that so many protest movements come to nothing. The Si Se Puede immigration reform protests, occurring regularly across our country in the first decade of this millennia, have not resulted in any meaningful legislative or social progress. The Occupy Movement protests, which commanded so much attention at first in 2011, did not lead to any concrete solutions to the problems of income inequality and seemed to fizzle out. Many Americans vigorously protested against going to war during the lead-up to the conflict in Iraq. We went anyway. The Arab

Spring uprisings throughout the Middle East seem only to have served as the match that lit a horrific fire.

So, we're not sure about the value of becoming a protestor. We're not sure it's going to work. We're not sure it's going to be safe. We're not sure that it won't stereotype us as something we're not.

And, of course, we can't be sure about any of those things. What we can do is look at the history of protesting, and see that effective protest movements have certain things in common.

Firstly, effective protests are peaceful. This is especially true if you are protesting against violence! Duh! But wherever there is protest, there is passion. And, where there is passion, sometimes people get violent. During the Vietnam era, protests proved to be a potent tool to end the war, especially as the size of the crowds and the number of protests increased dramatically. But throughout that period, the effectiveness of the protest movement was compromised by frequent violent outbursts among the protesters. That gave the "hawks" ammunition to discount and discredit the anti-war movement.

Political scientist Erica Chenoweth looked at hundreds of violent and non-violent movements that occurred from 1900-2006 to overthrow governments or demand territorial liberation. She found that non-violent campaigns were much more likely to be successful.

As we all know, Dr. Martin Luther King was our nation's chief proponent of peaceful and non-violent protest. He insisted that peaceful protest was the only way forward, even in the face of so much pressure to resort to violence. He famously said, "They cannot become who they need to become, unless we become who we need to become."

> *If we are going to protest for the cause of peace, we need to be committed to protesting peacefully.*

If we are going to protest for the cause of peace, we need to be committed to protesting peacefully. We need to reject and denounce all and any who believe in our cause, but are not committed to non-violence.

Secondly, effective protest movements have clear, well-articulated, concise, and limited demands. The anti-Soviet protests in Eastern Europe during the 1990s were effective because their message was clear and easily understood… Soviets get out! The civil rights era protests prevailed because everyone knew what the protestors wanted, and it wasn't hard to understand…equal access and equal voting rights. No one wondered what the antiwar protestors of the late 60s and early 70s were demanding. It was simple…get out of Vietnam.

By contrast, the Occupy Movement struggled to articulate one or two clear demands. Its ultimate aim was understandable enough…end income inequality. But the means to get there were vague, complicated, and too multi-faceted. Were they asking for banking industry regulations? Yes, but what were they, and how could you explain these complex regulations to the general public? Were they asking for a Robin Hood tax? Well yes, some of them. But others had different ideas about what needed to be done. There was no unanimity among the occupiers themselves, and they could not articulate a common theme when they had an opportunity to talk to the press. Nobody was sure what they wanted. So the encampments came down one by one, and the movement largely faded from public awareness.

This fact gives us hope, because when we protest for peace, our demands are clear. Stop the violence. Stop the warmongering. Stop mischaracterizing and demonizing others. Not only are these goals easily understood, but they are clearly and undeniably just. That makes for an effective protest.

Thirdly, size matters! Effective protests occur when the crowds are large, the movement is widespread, and the participation is growing. It's hard to ignore a crowd of 1,000, or 10,000, or 100,000.

Again citing the work of Erica Chenowith, "Researchers used to say that no government could survive if just 5 percent of the population rose up against it," but it may actually be lower than that. "No single campaign [within the scope of her study period of 1900–2006] failed after they'd achieved the active and sustained participation of just 3.5 percent of the population."

On September 11, 1988, a massive song festival, called Song of Estonia, was held at the Tallinn Song Festival Arena. It was a remarkable "singing revolution," with 300,000 Estonians (fully a quarter of the country's population) gathering to sing forbidden national hymns in the face of Soviet aggression. They sang together for hours. At that moment, the departure of the Soviets became inevitable.

Of course, every large movement starts out small. So a seemingly insignificant gathering of 10 or 15 or 20 protesters may at first seem ineffectual, or maybe even embarrassingly weak. But if the cause is just, and the tactics are peaceful, and the protesters are respectful, then you may find yourself on the ground floor of a movement that captures the moral soul of a nation.

5. GO OVERSEAS ON A SHORT-TERM DEVELOPMENT PROJECT

For an American, third-world travel always includes a big dose of reality. It kind of hits you right in the face. This is especially true when your travels put you in direct contact with local people who are living the real problems about society.

Traveling with a church group or a development agency to an impoverished region for the purpose of participating in a project designed to improve quality-of-life can be an unparalleled way to promote peace and become a better peacemaker.

Frequently on these trips, you spend a lot of time being uncomfortable. Unless you're from a humid region in the United States, you may discover that the humid air hits you like a wall as soon as you step off the airplane. You feel like you're trying to breath mushroom soup.

Typically on these kinds of trips, you eat rough, sleep rough, and travel rough. It's a real adventure. As I always say after going to a remote place, Indiana Jones got nothin' on me.

Exposure to that level of poverty can be staggering. Often you will encounter people who are dirt poor. Literally, they have nothing but dirt. They may live in mud huts, and their only possessions are items hand fashioned out of whatever they can find in the environment. They may be drinking dirty water, or in some cases have no water, requiring them to hike for miles every day. They survive on subsistence farming. You become amazed at what people are willing to do to survive and amazed at what people are able to tolerate when they have to.

For each of the last 35 years, I have taken groups to Mexico, Kenya, or Guatemala. It's always fascinating for me to watch the reaction of those who are having this experience for the first time. In almost every case, they will say something like, "This is unreal!" And then at some point on the trip, they realize it's life in the United States that isn't real. The place where we live is the unreal place. In most places around the world, and in most times of history, people have lived like the impoverished people whom we are visiting.

Only over the course of the last century have we built this Western Disneyland where we live. Here in our country, we wallow in comfort and excess—which are the very things that give us a perspective on our lives and the lives of others that simply isn't real. We hide away the kind of suffering and pain that exists openly on the streets in third-world countries. It isn't really that there is less suffering here; it's just that we don't see it. And when we fail to see suffering, it greatly limits our motivation to be peacemakers.

So we need to get real about the nature of comfort and discomfort and begin to understand the disadvantages and advantages that each bring to life. When you are on a development trip, you begin to realize how integral comfort has become to our lives, and how addicted we are to comfort. Comfort has become a kind of god for us. We worship being comfortable, and we don't realize how addicted we are to comfort until we get to a place where we are routinely uncomfortable.

Here in the West, we suffer from what I call the "Goldilocks Syndrome." We like it not too hot, not too cold, not too hard, not too soft. It's got to be "just right" for us.

When you travel and live amidst real, third-world conditions, you begin to realize that humans aren't born with a need to be comfortable. It's just not normal that people would be comfortable all the time. It's not how human beings have lived in the past, and it's not how most human beings live now. It's not how life was meant to be lived.

This need to be comfortable all the time is something bred into us by the Western life, and it robs us of some things. It denies us certain joys we're not even aware of. It makes us lose track of the fact that there are more important things in this world than being comfortable.

When you're willing to live with personal discomfort and sacrifice, it makes you much more open to the kinds of compromises and sacrifices that are necessary for peace to flourish.

The thing about being comfortable is that if you get too comfortable, you tend to fall asleep. And that's what's happened to us here in the West. We have fallen asleep. We are living in a moral and spiritual stupor. The experience of being uncomfortable comes with a gift. It gives the gift of awakening.

This kind of travel helps us to get real about the seriousness of *our* situation here in the first world. We go to these places thinking we are there to help people who are living in poverty. And we are. But it also helps us to see how dire our own situation is. We need to get real about how much danger we are in, and it's not about the things that we typically think are dangerous.

We need to get real about the serious danger that materialism poses to our soul. Jesus was very vocal about this. He said: "What good does it do to gain the whole world and lose your soul?" *(Mark 8:36)* And that's what we're doing here in the West. We have gained so much, but we've lost much more in the process.

We need to get real about the serious danger that poverty poses in our world. When the majority of the world is very, very poor, and a small few are very, very rich, and the rich keep getting richer, and the poor getting poorer… that is extremely dangerous. This imbalance destabilizes the world and makes it unsafe. And the rich will not survive it.

We need to get real about the serious danger that we, as Westerners, do not know how to suffer well. We are wimps and whiners. We are babies. Get a little hot, a little hungry, a little dirty, a little uncomfortable, and we can't hack it. The poor show us how to suffer well, with dignity, grace, faith… even joy.

In the Western world, we are materially rich, but spiritually poor. In the third world, most everyone is materially poor, but spiritually rich. Now you tell me…who do you think is better off?

Once I was in Kenya on a 30-seat bus taking 60 kids on a beach trip. It was the first time any of them had ever been out of their small rural village, though the beach was only 30 miles away. They were so excited that they were coming out of their skins.

As I stood in the aisle of the bus, I felt a tug on my shirt. I leaned down to hear what a tiny 10-year-old child wanted to tell me. She said to me, "I think we are really rich." I was dumbfounded. I didn't know what to say. It made me want to cry. This child who had nothing, thought of herself as rich. It is for her and countless others who encourage me in my pursuit to do whatever I can to bring peace.

These kinds of encounters have helped me to realize that the struggle for peace is not mostly about nations or tribes or communities. It's not mostly about devastation on a grand scale, engulfing millions of nameless, faceless people whom I have never met. It's about individuals I know personally. It's about little children. It's about beautiful people whose lives matter. And that makes me want to fight for peace and justice with every ounce of passion and courage I have.

When I hear about a bombing in Mombasa or gang violence in Guatemala, I think immediately about people I know personally. Even when events take place in countries where I have never traveled, it makes me think about real people in real places. If we can't do that, then we can never be effective, motivated peacemakers. Peacemakers have to think about consequences for individuals, not threats from the masses.

I want my kids to live in a more peaceful world. I want my grandchildren to inherit a more hopeful future. But if I'm just thinking about my kids and my grandkids, that won't help me to foster peace. If I'm just looking out for "me and mine," then I will actually be making the world worse for my kids and grandkids. I need to think about everybody's kids and everybody's grandkids.

So many people in our world have become radicalized. They have been driven by poverty or racism or fanaticism to violence and hatred toward other human beings. But it is now time for a different type of radicalization. It is time for us to truly follow the most radical human being who ever lived. The Prince of Peace.

This is how I try to live my life. I encourage you to do the same.

What Good, Small, Faithful Step Can I Take to Encourage Peace?

I am going to step away from my everyday comforts long enough to see that the world needs peacemakers like me to bring about lasting goodness and change.

I I I

Encouraging Peace:
An Overview

What Good, Small, Faithful Steps Can I Take to Encourage Peace?

I can be a calm, quiet diplomat in
a crowd of angry cowboys.

■ ■ ■

I can see that my Christian worldview is narrow and that to
bring peace, I must seek wisdom and act with humility.

■ ■ ■

I can learn to play nice, realizing that I don't
have to be right every single time.

■ ■ ■

When I have hurt someone, I am going to be a
courageous big boy or big girl and ask for forgiveness.

■ ■ ■

I can ignore those who spread fear and hatred
across my country and instead embrace every
challenge as an opportunity to be great.

■ ■ ■

I will not talk smack about other religions or nationalities, knowing that Jesus has called us to love *all* people.

I will cross the road, and go out of my way to make peace by making friends and establishing ongoing relationships with people who have a different racial make-up than I do.

I am going to step away from my everyday comforts long enough to see that the world needs peacemakers like me to bring about lasting goodness and change.

About the Author

Mark Traylor is the founder and pastor of Eastwind Community Church, a nondenominational church in Boise, Idaho, where he has served for 21 years. Mark is passionate about bringing together people with diverse attitudes, beliefs, and politics. He has built a congregation that is accepting and non-judgmental, where Democrats and Republicans have become great friends, and where people are encouraged to overcome fear and distrust through understanding.

NO TREES WERE HARMED IN THE MAKING OF THIS BOOK.

OK, so a few did make the ultimate sacrifice.

In order to steward our environment, we are partnered with *Plant With Purpose*, to plant a tree for every tree that paid the price for the printing of this book.

To learn more, visit www.elevatepub.com/about